SU-100

SELF-PROPELLED GUN

CONTENTS

Red Machines Vol.2 SU-100 Self-Propelled Gun

©Canfora Publishing 2020
ISBN 978-91-984775-8-0
Project Manager: James Kinnear
Design: Toni Canfora
Print: Printbest, Tallinn, Estonia

Canfora Publishing/Canfora Grafisk Form
Upplandsgatan 96A
113 44 Stockholm, Sweden
www.canfora.se
info@canfora.se

INTRODUCTION

The Samokhodnaya Ustanovka* - 100 (Self-Propelled Gun - 100mm), also known as a Samokhodnaya Artilleriskaya Ustanovka (SAU), or Self-Propelled Gun (SPG) in English - is a well known Soviet World War Two tank destroyer, the relatively short combat history of which has been well covered at a superficial level in Western books and articles.

Due to its late entry into the Second World War and the fact that SU-100s today preserved in museum collections are a mix of late wartime, post-war Soviet and post-war Czechoslovakian production, the history of the wartime production SU-100, its production derivatives and the changes introduced during production have historically been devoid of detail and specific dates. There has also been considerable conflation between wartime and post-war production changes, which has been unfortunate and confusing for military historians and modellers alike. This book for the first time details from primary Russian sources the complete development of the SU-100 and provides the timelines during which almost constant changes in production were undertaken. It also relates the combat service of the SU-100 in the Red Army, the post-war Soviet Army and the armies of the Warsaw Pact, and service with Soviet client states in many other areas of the world.

This book concentrates primarily on the Soviet built SU-100, beginning with the development of the SU-100 and its production at the Ural Heavy Machine Building Plant (known variously as UZTM, Uralmash or Uralmashzavod) in Sverdlovsk**. Less well known, the SU-100 was also later built as an interim production measure at Plant №174 in Omsk. Post-war, the SU-100 was modernised several times, and was also assembled in Czechoslovakia as the SD-100, the latter country being the producer of nearly all the self-propelled guns of this type captured in Middle East wars and displayed in military museums as "Russian" SU-100s.

---

* Ustanovka directly translates as "unit" or "installation" rather than gun, hence technically SU or SAU refers to a self propelled "unit" but the Russian meaning is self-propelled gun or artillery piece.

** The Siberian city of Ekaterinburg was renamed Sverdlovsk in 1924 and became a major military production centre. Sverdlovsk reverted to its earlier pre-Soviet name of Ekaterinburg after the break-up of the Soviet Union in 1991.

Chapter 1

The Ural Heavy Machine Building Plant (UZTM)
- Uralmashzavod

The Ural Heavy Machine Building Plant (UZTM), also known as Uralmashzavod, was founded in the city of Sverdlovsk in 1933. The massive plant was, as the name rather implicitly implied, concentrated on the production of heavy machinery for other metallurgical plants, such as blast furnace equipment and machinery for processing and forming ferrous and non-ferrous metals. At the end of the decade the plant also began to become more directly involved in military manufacture. In addition to the armoured vehicles for which the plant would become famous, Artillery Plant №9 where F.F. Petrov was chief designer was at the time also loca-

ted within the UZTM structure. Plant №9 developed weapons such as the 122mm M-30 howitzer, which was modified for use in the first UZTM self-propelled gun design, the SU-122. By the time the SU-100 was under development, UZTM had considerable direct and indirect experience in both the chassis and armament components of armoured vehicle production, with all required facilities located within a single Siberian city and its immediate environs.

With the outbreak of war and the mass evacuation of Soviet military manufacturing capability to safety beyond the Ural mountains, UZTM in Sverdlovsk received tooling evacu-

Armament complete with gun mantlet being installed in later production SU-100s at UZTM (Vyacheslav Belogrud).

SU-100s wrapped in tarpaulins being shipped by rail from directly within the UZTM plant in the winter of 1944-1945. The box bolted to the hull rear under the tarpaulin is a solid fuel heater container, shipped pre-attached in the winter months only.

The SU-100 assembly line at UZTM. These are later production vehicles with the enlarged commander's cupola and other detail changes.

ated from other plants in danger of being overrun, and began to produce complete hull and turret armour sets for the T-34 medium tank. The plant then adapted the base T-34 chassis to mount the 122mm M-30 howitzer as the SU-122, which was soon thereafter followed by the SU-85 and the final wartime tank destroyer mounted on the T-34 chassis, the SU-100.

Post war, Uralmashzavod was reorganised and significantly enlarged, but it returned to primarily civilian production, concentrating on the manufacture of drilling rigs for the oil industry, milling equipment, and various hydraulic presses and other capital machine tools. After the fall of the Soviet Uni-

on in 1991, the plant became the "The Ural Heavy Machine Building Plant Open Joint Stock Company" which was still abbreviated to "UZTM". In 1996 the company merged into the "OMZ" plant, and in 2005 the Russian gas company Gazprom - one of the plant's major clients, bought a controlling share in the company. The Ural Heavy Machine Building Plant, usually abbreviated to UZTM, has thereby been known by several different names during its long history, all of which are interchangeable. The original full UZTM designation was often abbreviated to the "Uralskiy Mashinostroitelniy Zavod" (Urals Machine Building Plant) - minus the "heavy" - and was frequently referred to as "Uralmashzavod" (the Urals Machinery Plant) or simply as "Uralmash" (Urals Machinery....) using a typical Russian incomplete short-form trait of not completing a sentence as it was understood that it was a "Zavod" or production plant, which is well understood among Russians but sometimes baffles outsiders. The "Uralmash" plant was also for a short period designated as the Ural Heavy Machinery Plant named after Ordzhonikidze, in deference to the Russian revo-

lutionary of Georgian origin who was a long-term comrade of Stalin and among other posts held was in the early 1930s the Commissar for Heavy Industry.

All the terms, as often intermixed and sometimes conflated, refer to the same manufacturing plant located in Sverdlovsk, today Ekaterinburg, in the Urals region on the borders of European Russia and Siberia.

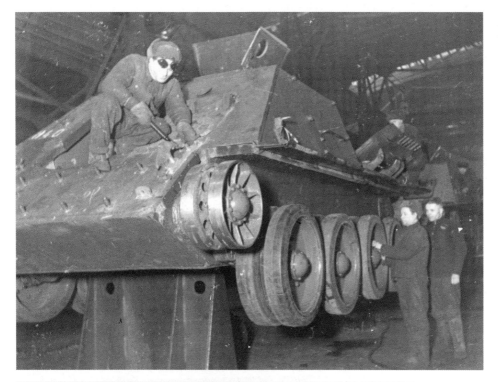

Electric arc welding fitments on the SU-100 casemate hull. Note the assembly stand.

An SU-100 awaiting installation of the engine, transmission and final drives.

A V-2 engine being installed in a nearly complete SU-100 during assembly.

Chapter 2

SU-100 Prototypes

From September 1942 until August 1943, Uralmashzavod (UZTM) was primarily concerned with the production of T-34 medium tanks; however in November 1942 it also began to assemble a self-propelled howitzer on the T-34 chassis which was both designed and produced within the Uralmashzavod plant. The new self-propelled howitzer was armed with a modification of the 122mm M-30 towed divisional howitzer mounted in a new casemate housing on the T-34 chassis. The new SAU, designated SU-122, began to be assembled in December 1942, and was detailed in UZTM records simply as a "samokhod" or self-propelled artillery piece - usually abbreviated to SAU. Although the SU-122 was an effective close-support weapon, the rapid advancement of wartime armaments required the deployment of a more specific tank destroyer, which was duly developed on a modified casemate chassis using experience gained with the SU-122. The new SAU, designated SU-85, entered production at UZTM in July 1943, armed with the 85mm D-5S-85 gun, the same D-5 series weapon as mounted in the early T-34-85 medium tank as the D-5T, adapted as the D-5S for use in an SAU.

The new SU-85 was officially accepted for service with the Red Army in accordance with GKO (State Defence Committee) Resolution №3892ss dated 7th August 1943, a month after assembly of the SU-85 had already started at the plant, as was the trailing bureaucratic norm in the wartime Soviet Union. The same resolution cancelled production of the SU-122 and also T-34 medium tank production at the plant, in order that Uralmash henceforth concentrate on SAU production. From August 1943 UZTM thereby became the default Soviet "samokhod" or SAU production plant, in addition to continuing production of T-34 tank components for other plants assembling T-34 line tanks.

In November 1943, with the SU-85 in full series production at UZTM, a meeting was held with representatives of MVTU (Moscow Technical University), UZTM and the Technical Command of the NKV (the People's Commissariat of Armaments) at which it was decided that from a rational viewpoint the optimum resolution for combatting newly emerging German tanks would be for future Soviet tanks to be armed with 100-107mm calibre main armament. Consideration had in September 1943 been given to arming the existing SU-85 with the 122mm M-1943 (D-25) gun or the 152mm M-1943 (D-15) howitzer as the SU-D-25 and SU-D-15 respectively; however the use of a 100mm calibre weapon was consi-

The first prototype SU-100 had many components borrowed directly from the T-34, such as the commander's cupola and the track guards. The gun mantlet lacks the distinctive grooves in the fixed mantlet section casting that were later added for convenience in locating the mounting bolts. The tow cable hook locations are unique to the prototype, and the wheels have rims with 42 perforation holes, production of which type was suspended in April 1944.

The first prototype SU-100 located outside the UZTM plant.

dered more suitable for a medium tank chassis based self-propelled gun primarily geared towards a tank support role. Such a weapon was already available, in the form of the 100mm B-34 naval gun, which could be adapted for use on tanks and SAUs. The corresponding Commissariat of Armaments (NKV) order was issued on 11th November 1943. However, to design an entirely new weapon and associated ammunition for a new calibre proved more complex under wartime conditions than developing a new weapon from scratch.

At Uralmash, chief designer L.I. Gorlitsky had meantime already developed a new SAU design as a plant initiative. Working with his team which included G. F. Ksunin and A. G. Gaivoronsky (motor group), A. D. Nekhludov (hull design), V. L. Likhomanov (electrics), L. A. Pinosol (drawings) and others, Gorlitsky developed the preliminary design of the new SAU based on the existing SU-85 chassis, to be armed with a 100mm tank gun - the D-10S - then being developed locally by Plant №9. The plans were sent to the People's Commissariat of the Tank Industry (NarKomat Tankovoi Promishlennosti - NKTP) and the Self-Propelled Artillery Command (USA). After review, the State Defence Committee (GKO) issued Resolution №4851, which sanctioned the arming of the new IS-2 heavy tank and "medium" SAUs with the new 100mm armament.

However, as Gorlitsky's team at Uralmash worked on their plant initiative design, which envisaged using the 100mm D-10S gun being developed within the plant structure, a directive was received from the People's Commissariat of the Tank Industry (NKTP). Order №765, dated 28th December 1943, which obligated Uralmashzavod to before 15th January 1944, design an SAU on the T-34 medium tank chassis suitable for installation of the 100mm S-34 gun developed by TsAKB (the Central Artillery Design Bureau). This was a major blow to the Uralmash initiative, as TsAKB, located in the Moscow suburb

of Kaliningrad (today Korolev) was responsible for all artillery development in the Soviet Union, and was headed by the famous Soviet artillery designer V. G. Grabin. The same Grabin also led his own plant design team at Plant №92 in Gorky which was in favour of the 100mm S-34 conversion from the B-34 naval gun. The 100mm D-10S was in danger of being a stillborn design.

By the same Order №765, UZTM was instructed to complete a plant prototype of the new SAU before 20th February 1944 - to be armed with the 100mm S-34 gun, which was to be provided to Uralmashzavod by Plant №92 before 25th January 1944. State trials of the SU-100 prototype were to be completed by 25th February, five days after the prototype was to be fully assembled. However, on receiving the 100mm S-34 drawings from TsAKB in Sverdlovsk, it was confirmed by the SAU designers at UZTM (as had always been clear to them)

The first prototype SU-100 self propelled gun alongside the earlier SU-85 during UZTM plant trials. Both SAUs were based on the chassis of the UZTM production T-34. The main tactical role of the SU-100, as with the earlier SU-85, was as a tank destroyer.

that the S-34, originally designed for mounting in a naval gun turret where space was not at a premium, would be near-impossible to install within a T-34 based casemate chassis. The gun breech mechanism and the gun mounting were particularly wide, and the gun would strike the internal suspension spring casing for the second road wheel station when traversed to the left. Furthermore there was insufficient space to mount a driver-mechanic's hatch in the glacis plate, with even a half-hatch as used on the SU-122 being an impractical proposition. To install the 100mm S-34 gun in the new SAU prototype would involve major modification to the casemate hull design and new suspension geometry. This would in turn require major re-tooling of the production machinery at UZTM, including fabrication of new hull assembly welding stands, notwithstanding the problem of altering the front suspension layout and road wheel spacing to cope with the added weight. It would also be neces-

SU-100 first prototype. Note that the prototype had only a single turret ventilator dome on the fighting compartment roof. The tracks were cast by workshop №110 within UZTM.

sary to move the driver-mechanic's position and all his controls 100mm to the left, resulting in him being cramped between the hull side armour and the armament, which would hamper his ability to control the vehicle adequately. The 100mm S-34 installation would also require extending the upper casemate out to what were the outer edges of the track guards on the SU-85, together with other changes that would add 3.5 metric tonnes to the combat weight of the new SAU as compared with the SU-85. Worse, the hull and casemate modifications required were so extensive that the standard T-34 "Christie" type suspension of the SU-85 would need to be changed for torsion bar suspension, effectively requiring an entirely new SAU design, a highly impractical proposition during wartime.

Inevitably, despite the not inconsequential engineering issues, TsAKB took the same familiar "departmental position" that it had taken when the SU-85 was in development, demanding that the 100mm S-34 was to be mounted in the existing SU-85 chassis without modification, whether it was an impractically tight fit or not. This was clearly a far from ideal - or even logical - situation, but a repeating Soviet theme where politics and engineering collided. The solution was however the same as that used to win the argument on the earlier SU-85 design. UZTM went back to Plant №9 NKV, also located in Sverdlovsk, which had assisted UZTM before in providing an engineering solution that resolved the earlier dispute with TsAKB over the SU-85. The armament designers at Plant №9 under the direction of another famous artillery designer, F.F. Petrov, worked with Gorlitsky's engineers at UZTM to create a 100mm gun which in all respects met the original design specification objectives defined for the S-34, but in a neater installation more appropriate for use in an armoured vehicle. The "new" weapon developed at Plant №9 was designated the 100mm D-10S (S-Samokhodnaya - self propelled), and was effectively the weapon which the plant had already been working on before the TsAKB debacle started. It had near identical ballistics to the 100mm S-34 gun, but could be installed in the existing SU-85 chassis with minimal changes to the casemate armour and no major modifications to the base chassis, while not significantly adding to the overall combat weight of the new SU-100. With a bit of subterfuge, it looked as if UZTM would be able to build the SU-100 as envisaged in the original plant initiative.

There were at the time no Tactical and Technical Conditions (TTUs) in place for the new SAU, so these were completed internally within UZTM on 10th January 1944; these TTUs being subsequently adopted as the general requirements of the design of the SU-100.

The Tactical and Technical Specifications (TTKh) stated that the main purpose of the new SAU was to destroy heavy

The SU-100 first prototype. Note the long handrails on both sides of the casemate hull, which were shortened on the second prototype and the series production SU-100. The tow cables are of standard 4 metre length T-34 tank type. Note the use of castellated nuts on the drive sprockets.

tanks and SPGs with an armour thickness of 100-150mm from medium ranges of 800-1,500m. The Tactical and Technical Requirements (TTTs) meantime were based on the following basic specifications:

1) *Use of the serial production SU-85 chassis.*

2) *Armament to be the 100mm D-10S gun manufactured by Plant №9 NKV.*

3) *A 1.5 tonne permissible increase in SAU combat weight over the series production SU-85 (to 31 metric tonnes).*

4) *An increase in frontal hull and casemate glacis armour thickness to 75mm.*

5) *To maximise visibility, fitment of Mk.4 vision devices and a commander's cupola.*

6) *Due to some overloading on the front road wheels, increase the front suspension spring steel diameter from 30mm to 34mm.*

In answering for its own internally generated specifications before the Commissariat for the Tank Industry (NKTP) on 11th January, UZTM reported that the TsAKB preference for main armament in the SU-100 (the 100mm S-34) was not technically appropriate, and that UZTM had chosen the 100mm D-10S developed by Plant №9 NKV as the better option for the SU-100. The findings were followed by a long and detailed report on both alternative armament proposals and a conclusion as to how UZTM had come to that technical decision. As a result, UZTM was permitted to build a prototype for evaluation purposes, which was duly completed at Uralmashzavod in February 1944. Plant trials included the firing of 30 rounds of ammunition, and a 150km mobility test on differing surfaces, during which there were no mechanical failures. The prototype was passed for state trials, and was sent to the Gorokhovets artillery polygon on 3rd March. The state trials were successful and on 14th April UZTM was given the formal order to start series production of the SU-100 self-propelled gun. Theoretically, the correct design solution had been found and accepted, the prototype manufactured and accepted for service following state trials, and the requirements of the GKO resolution dated 28th December 1943 implemented. However, TsAKB, and specifically its head, V.G. Grabin, insisted that the original specifications of the GKO resolution should nevertheless be implemented in full; namely UZTM was obliged to build an SU-100 prototype armed with a 100mm S-34 gun, as originally demanded by Grabin himself in his position as head of TsAKB - which had the ultimate authority of all matters related to artillery design. It appeared that UZTM had been outflanked by Grabin and his team at Plant №92, and with Grabin also being the head of TsAKB, there was little that UZTM could do - formally - but comply with their direct orders.

The receipt by Uralmash of the appropriate formal directives requiring the plant to carry out the TsAKB instructions triggered two months of correspondence between TsAKB and the reluctant UZTM designers as to how the bulkier 100mm S-34 should be installed. Ultimately, Plant №100 in Chelyabinsk (producing the IS-2 heavy tank) sent UZTM an existing 100mm S-34 tank gun on 20th April for test-fit purposes. Two days later, on 22nd April, a telegram was sent to the People's Commissar for Tank Industry (NKTP) by UZTM - doubtless with some unexpressed glee - confirming that the 100mm S-34 would as predicted not fit, surprisingly, in the prototype SU-100 chassis; hence the gun would need to be modified at an artillery manufacturing plant in accordance with design changes, that UZTM would of course need to specify. The game of "shakhmati" (chess) between the design bureaus continued.

SU-100-2 Prototype (100mm S-34)

On 30th April a combined order from the People's Commissar of the Tank Industry (NKTP), the People's Commissar of Armament (NKV), the Main Artillery Directorate (GAU) and the Command of the Armoured and Motorised Forces (BTiMV) of the Red Army required UZTM to by 8th May 1944 assemble a prototype SU-100 self-propelled gun armed with the 100mm S-34, notwithstanding the protests from UZTM regarding the practicalities of making it fit within the SU-100 chassis and casemate. On completion of plant trials, UZTM was directed to by 10th May dispatch the prototype to the Gorokhovets artillery polygon to undergo the same state trials previously undertaken with the original prototype SU-100 armed with the 100mm D-10S gun, for comparative evaluation of the two SU-100 prototypes with their alternative armament options.

Work on the "alternative" S-34 armed SU-100 proceeded far from smoothly, and on 3rd May 1944, NKTP provided a final deadline of 10th May for production of the self-propelled gun armed with the 100mm S-34 gun. UZTM replied that the armament could be installed within twelve days; however, the installation would require radical modification of the armament at the providing artillery plant prior to shipment to UZTM. Finally, Artillery Plant №9 received an order to partly revise the 100mm S-34 in accordance with UZTM requirements, consisting of the following:

1) Decrease the gun cradle width by 160mm.
2) Produce new gun mounting mandrels.
3) Remove the machine gun embrasure.
4) Produce a new frame, rotating mechanism and travel lock.
5) Produce a new sight mounting.

The changes required were stated as the minimum needed to produce a workable S-34 gun without completely altering the design. Complete removal of all the noted defects would lead to the S-34 gun becoming effectively an exact copy of the D-10S as already developed by Plant №9 which TsAKB was undermining with their S-34 preference.

The new SU-100 prototype built using a modified S-34 gun was given the index SU-100-2. Accordingly, the earlier D-10S armed first prototype can be accorded the designation SU-100-1, but it was not so designated in documents. As the SU-100-2 armed with the (much modified) S-34 was being assembled, the second prototype SU-100 armed with the 100mm D-10S was also being completed, and was tested before the SU-100-2. In accordance with an NKTP order dated 26th May, UZTM was required to finish the second SU-100 prototype armed with D-10S gun before 27th June, and by 1st July was to present it for state trials. However, because the 100mm D-10S armed design differed little from the series production SU-85 and was a modification of the original SU-100 prototype, the plant completed the prototype ten days early, and state testing was held at the Gorokhovets polygon from 24th to 28th June.

The SU-100-2 armed with the TsAKB 100mm S-34 gun was delivered to the Gorokhovets polygon by a special train in early July 1944, and tested by the same state commission that had days before tested the second SU-100 prototype armed with the 100mm D-10S. Somewhat ironically, the commission found the 100mm S-34 armed SU-100-2 to be inferior in many respects to the SU-100 armed with the 100mm D-10S gun built by Plant №9. The SU-100-2 was thereby not recommended for acceptance in the Red Army. So ended the déjà vu

---

* ANIOP - Artillerisky Nauchno-Issledovatelsky Opitny Polygon Glavnogo Artilleriiskogo Upravleniya - Artillery Scientific Research Experimental Polygon of the Main Artillery Directorate. **(TsAMO Fund 38, Inventory 11369, Case 289).

The first prototype SU-100 during state trials conducted from 9th-27th March 1944 at the ANIOP GAU Gorokhovets proving grounds. The photographs clearly illustrate the difficulties for the driver-mechanic in avoiding damage to the 100mm D-10S gun when crossing ditches and rough terrain.

story that had previously unfolded with the SU-85, with the same competition between gun designs from the competing TsAKB and Plant №9 plants and the same ultimate outcome. The arguments had however significantly delayed the beginning of SU-100 series production.

The design improvements introduced on the first and second SU-100 prototypes armed with the 100mm D-10S gun are set out below in chronological order.

SU-100 First Prototype (100mm D-10S) - February 1944

The first SU-100 prototype, armed with the 100mm gun D-10S produced at Plant №9 NKV was completed at Sverdlovsk in January 1944. The prototype successfully passed plant trials in February 1944, and was from 9th to 27th March tested at the Gorokhovets Artillery Polygon of the Main Artillery Directorate (ANIOP GAU)*, after which the state commission headed by Colonel Repishev concluded that:

"100mm SU with the gun D-100 (so called D-10S gun in this document) after field test firing of 1,040 rounds, of which 517 rounds were with enhanced charge, and completing 564km of mobility trials, and after the elimination of all defects referred to in this report, in the Commission's opinion after these prototype tests may be recommended to the Red Army (for service acceptance)."

In the commission's opinion, the following design improvements were required:

1) A lock on the electric gun trigger was required to eliminate the potential for accidentally firing the gun.
2) The commander's working space required improvement.
3) The mounting of the armament in travelling (locked) position needed improvement.
4) Ventilation in the fighting compartment needed improvement.
5) The fastening of stowed ammunition needed revisions.
6) The engine crankshaft grease should be changed to "aviation" lubricant.
7) The hatch covers and ventilator cap needed improvement.

Among other instructions there was a rare Soviet wartime "aesthetic" requirement to eliminate the ledge of the upper front part of the hull glacis above the front beam, resulting from the increase in the thickness of the frontal glacis armour from 45mm to 75mm. The use of a cast beam connecting the upper and lower frontal armour plates - carried over from the T-34 tank and the SU-85 - remained unchanged. The SU-100

was produced in this form until May 1945, as modifying the tooling to produce modified beam sections was impractical under wartime conditions.

The first prototype had minimal external differences from the SU-85 as then being produced at UZTM. The gun mantlet was almost identical but had increased 150mm armour thickness. The casemate hull was identical but for the increased thickness of the frontal armour to 75mm. The commander's visibility was greatly improved. The commander's position instead of having a raised section with two mirror periscopes as on the SU-85 now featured a distinctive commander's "conning tower", fitted with a cupola taken from the T-34 and providing 360° visibility by means of multiple vision blocks. The later production SU-100 featured a "conning tower" with variable armour thickness (and which was not exactly circular in cross section) and a modified hemispherical cap for the ventilator fan as used on the early SU-85 and standard T-34.*

For locking the gun in travel position, the first prototype used a pivoting clamp attached directly to the inner roof section of the conning tower. It thereby did not have an armoured section on the fighting compartment roof for the gun detent lock system which was a feature of production SU-100s. When the armament was unlocked and in the firing position, it was thereby important for the crew to lock the bracket with a locking pin so it was not hanging freely, as otherwise it could cause injury during gun recoil.

SU-100 Second Prototype (100mm D-10S) - May 1944

The second prototype SU-100 was built incorporating the improvements recommended by the testing commission after trials of the first prototype. The second prototype also passed state trials at the ANIOP polygon near Gorokhovets, undertaken from 24th to 27th June. The commission, chaired by a Colonel Repishev noted that the second prototype of the SU-100 incorporated almost all the modifications recommended by the commission after testing of the first prototype. Modifications included:

1) Use of a manual hydraulic oil fill pump reinstated.
2) Introduction of servo springs in the drive of the main clutch.
3) Improvement of the commander's position, his seat and the location of the observation devices in the cupola.
4) Improved gun locking in the stowed position.
5) Improved ammunition fastening.
6) Introduction of an articulated telescopic gun sight.

---

* Self-Propelled Artillery (unit) SU-100. A brief technical description of the prototype model. June 1944. (TsAMO Fund 38, Inventory 11369, Case 460).

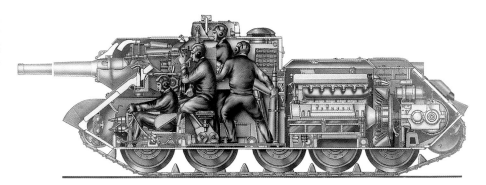

This plant illustration of the internal layout of the second prototype SU-100 shows features modified as a result of testing of the original prototype, such as the use of twin ventilator domes on the fighting compartment roof.

It was noted that with regard to the SU-100s tactical and technical data (weight, armour protection, mobility, fire power, rate of fire and manoeuvrability) the self-propelled gun met all current requirements for this type of weapon. Armament performance would ensure the successful defeat of modern enemy armour such as "Tiger" and "Panther" tanks at a range of 1,500m irrespective of the point of projectile impact. The heavily armoured "Ferdinand" self-propelled gun could also be defeated, but only with a direct hit to the side armour, albeit in this instance the engagement range could be as much as 2,000m. In conclusion it was stated that the UZTM plant's SU-100 self-propelled gun design, armed with the 100mm D-10S gun developed by Plant №9 NKV, was recommended for adoption by the Red Army, and that the stated deficiencies should be corrected and tested on the first series production self-propelled gun. The SU-100 self-propelled gun was thereby adopted for Red Army service by GKO Order №6131, dated 3rd July 1944, replacing the SU-85.

Among external visible changes on the second prototype in comparison with the first were:

1) Improved design of gun locking in the travelling position, with a small armoured raised "rubka" section appearing on the fighting compartment roof. The axis of the gun relative to the casemate roof was lowered by 10mm.

2) The 10T-15 telescopic sight as used in the series production SU-85 and the first prototype SU-100 was replaced by the TSh-15 articulated telescopic sight. The gun mantlet was slightly modified accordingly (the left side of the movable part of the mantlet was modified, the aperture for the sight

The second prototype SU-100 during state trials at the ANIOP GAU Gorokhovets proving grounds, conducted from 24th-27th June 1944. The commander's cupola with its variable thickness armour has been modified, as has the left side of the mantlet and its rain guard. The additional compressed air cylinder for engine start-up was stowed under the rear fuel tanks during trials only.

This photograph shows the second prototype SU-100 (right) being assembled alongside a standard SU-85 (left) at the UZTM plant. The later standard tandem turret ventilator dome is being welded in place on the second prototype.

was lowered, and the rain canopy modified, with an additional "overhang" above the left side of the mask).

3) The commander's cupola was moved further to the right from the central axis in order to provide better operating space, resulting in the sponson on the right side being further extended, most noticeable on the lower section.

4) The commander's cupola was now not taken directly from the T-34 and was asymmetrical in shape, with the frontal armour increased to 90mm, and with the viewing devices relocated.

5) Two new exhaust fans were mounted on the fighting compartment roof, with distinctive co-joined "bell" shaped armoured cupolas.

The fume extractor fans used on the production SU-100 were of a particularly distinctive design. At the initial design stage and during construction of the second prototype, the fans were covered by a pair of hemispherical "mushroom" caps as used on the T-34-85 produced at Plant №183 in Nizhny Tagil from March 1944. Plant №183 was the "parent" T-34 production plant

in the Urals region, and it dictated the layout and components used by other T-34 tank and T-34 related production plants. During testing the first SU-100 prototype additional "caps" for housing the electric fan motors had already been welded to the top of the standard "T-34" hemispherical cupolas. These were replaced by the distinctive "bell" shaped armoured fan covers on the second prototype, designed after feedback on testing of the original SU-100 prototype. The reasoning for spending so much effort on the construction of the extraction fans was again related to working space and clearances. After initial trials it was concluded that the fans needed to be modified and ideally moved closer to the gun breech, not least because with the gun at 3° depression and traversed 8° to the left the gun breech on recoil was dangerously close to damaging the MV-12 fan motor housings. The fans were thereby raised above the level of the fighting compartment roof, and located further into the cupolas, with the additional small "caps" being added for the relocated electric motors. On series production SU-100s, the now "bell" shaped fan cupolas were of cast rather than fabricated construction.

Side elevation and rear views of the second SU-100 prototype during trials at the ANIOP GAU polygon at Gorokhovets in late June 1944. The double ventilator motor housing caps fabricated for trials purposes were replaced with a cast assembly on the series production SU-100.

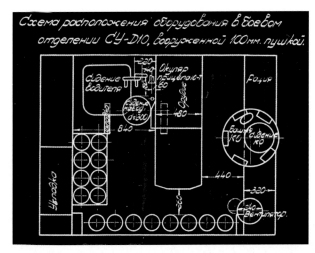

The first (above) and second (right) prototype fighting compartment layout schematics. Note the two exhaust fans and the added seat for gun loader.

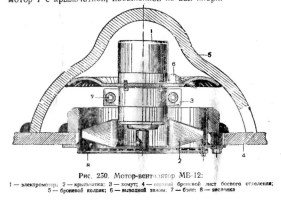

The MV-12 (Motor-Ventilator) of the series production SU-100 was mounted under an armoured bell-shaped housing which ensured that the moving parts of the fan did not intrude into the fighting compartment space.

The hemispherical armoured caps were modified on the second prototype during trials. Small caps were welded to the existing ventilators on the prototype to house the electric fan motors.

EhSU-100 Prototype

The KB at Uralmashzavod in collaboration with Plant N°627 in 1944 developed a prototype SU-100 with a similar electric transmission drive mechanism to that used on the German "Ferdinand" self-propelled gun. The prototype, designated EhSU-100, was developed under the direction of Eh. P. Stashinin as project leader. The EhSU-100 prototype was built in the summer of 1944 as the SU-100 was in the early stages of being prepared for series production. The EhSU-100 was together with other projects reviewed by the NKTP Technical Committee and senior state representatives. The commission concluded that the EhSU-100 incorporated *"progressive construction*

principles" but it was irrational to employ the mechanism on a medium SAU, especially as the electrical transmission mechanism added 3,000kg to the combat weight of the vehicle when compared with the use of a conventional mechanical gearbox. All work on the EhSU-100 was stopped in the autumn of 1944.

SU-85M

There was a three-month interval between the second prototype SU-100 successfully undergoing state trials and the start of SU-100 series production, as the SU-100 chassis and more particularly the 100mm D-10S ordnance were prepared for series production. The reason for this delay was that the modified

The gun mantlet on the first prototype SU-100 was similar in shape to that of the SU-85 with a new mounting bolt arrangement.

The second prototype gun mantlet. Clearly visible changes include enlargement of the left side of the mask. The TSh-15 gun sight porthole has been lowered, and the rain guard has been modified to accommodate the enlarged "cheekbone".

SU-100 chassis was ready for series production earlier than sufficient quantities of 100mm D-10S tank guns were available to mate to the chassis. Accordingly, in order to ensure minimum disruption to series production, L. I. Gorlitsky proposed that the 85mm D-5S and the new 100mm D-10S should both be mounted in the new common chassis according to armament (and more significantly, ammunition) availability. This resulted in the production of the interim SU-85M, an SU-85 mounting the 85mm D-5S gun in the new chassis and casemate hull developed for the SU-100M. The SU-85M was effectively a stopgap to utilise SU-100 chassis availability while quantities of 100mm D-10S guns were being made available to match chassis production.

The SU-85M was almost identical to the later 100mm D-10S armed SU-100, but for the shorter barrel and mantlet carried over from the SU-85. An advantage of the SU-85M using the new SU-100 hull was the increased ammunition complement of 60 rounds the new hull provided, together with significantly improved frontal armour protection.

The first SU-85M was completed in July 1944, with Uralmashzavod producing the "interim" SU-85M for three months from early August, with the SU-85M and later SU-100 latterly assembled alongside each other for a period of some weeks.

Comparing the gun mantlet of the first prototype SU-100 with the series production SU-85, the differences are minimal.

The SU-85M was short-lived as it was from the outset an interim production solution, and the 100mm D-10S provided a formidable increase in firepower. As delivery of 100mm tank guns - and new ammunition - increased, the SU-85's raison d'être evaporated.

The series production SU-85 armoured gun mantlet.

The series production SU-100 armoured gun mantlet.

The commander's cupola and sponson on the first prototype SU-100.

On the second SU-100 prototype, the location of the commander's cupola and sponson was moved slightly to the right relative to the first prototype, and the shape and location relative to the track guard is also not identical to the first prototype.

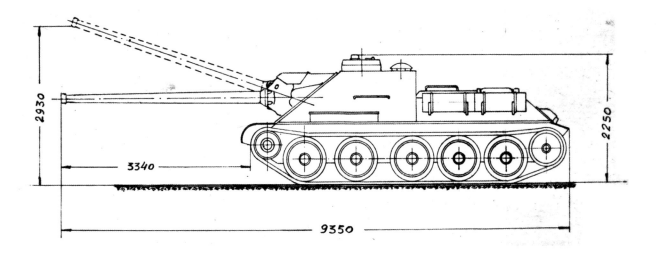

Soviet dimensional drawing of the second SU-100 prototype.

A column of SU-85Ms, 1st Belorussian Front, winter 1944-1945. The SU-85M and SU-100 were virtually indistinguishable from most angles, but the gun mantlet and its securing bolt pattern show this to be an SU-85M.

Chapter 3

Design Changes during SU-100 Series Production at UZTM

The SU-100, as with all Soviet armoured vehicles, was subject to numerous design revisions during its production life. The recent release of original blueprints and documents previously located within closed archives has however now allowed the entire production life of the SU-100 to be recounted in detail. The design information provided below has come from the following correlated sources:

1. The original design documentation, including production drawings from the Ural Heavy Machine Building Plant named after Ordzhonikidze, located in wartime Sverdlovsk (today Ekaterinburg). The plant as stated earlier is also known simply as Uralmash or abbreviated to UZTM. These drawings were in most cases transferred to the archives in the form of their latest revision, with all design changes incorporated as at the time of archiving. Drawing sets might thereby include 1944 or 1952 manufacture, and might incorporate upgrades made

even as late as in 1972, reflecting the ongoing process of update and modernisation.

2. The second source is surviving SU-100s preserved on pedestals or in museums, in instances where it has been possible to read the serial numbers. The serial number uniquely identifies the year and month of manufacture of any particular SU-100, and also whether it was the beginning or the end of the month when it was assembled. This gives an indication of the latest design changes that featured on any given hull and chassis as built. However, the wheels, tracks, lights, tool mountings, storage and other hull mounted equipment on these preserved SU-100s are almost always from a later date. The traces of welding, mounting points or ground-off location points also allow determination of what post-war upgrades were or were not undertaken on any particular SU-100.

The first production SU-100s were dispatched to the front

Early series production SU-100s in the UZTM plant yard. Sverdlovsk, autumn 1944.

in November 1944, with SU-100 losses in the final stage of the war being relatively small. The SU-100 remained in series production for some time after victory and some remained in service as training vehicles in the Soviet Army as late as the 1980s, so the survival rate of SU-100s which were neither destroyed in combat, nor later scrapped, is high relative to many other wartime era Soviet armoured vehicles.

The specifications of 36 known SU-100s surviving in the Russian Federation and countries of the former Soviet Union for which the serial numbers are evident were analysed in detail. This provided a "live" sample of Soviet SU-100s produced at UZTM during each month of 1945 and until February 1946, and as produced at Plant №174 in Omsk in May and July 1947, and in January 1948. According to the serial numbers on known surviving SU-100s, no early production SU-100s assembled in September-October 1944 would appear to have survived. As these SU-100s were used in combat at the front, these older and war-worn self-propelled guns (bearing in mind the distances they travelled in service) were quickly decommissioned post-war and scrapped, leaving the newer post-war production SU-100s in Soviet Army service, and later as the majority of museum relics.

3. Research was also conducted using a variety of available original reference archive materials. These included handwritten technical descriptions from the plant, test reports and test data, military acceptance trial reports, correspondence with the plant and the other material taken from documents in the TsAMO* archives. For anyone with a specific interest, background information including statistics on armour plate production scrap rates and other peripheral historical information is now in the public domain. An exceptional source of information would have been the "Prikaz Izmenenie Otdela Glavnogo Konstruktora" a listing of all the design changes ordered by the chief designer of the Uralmash plant, which governed all adjustments to the drawings and thereby changes introduced on series production SU-100s. Unfortunately, although more than six hundred of these orders were issued, covering everything from design changes to new methods of heat treatment or welding, and the make-up of materials or new internal parts, these Uralmash records have apparently not survived - or are yet to be found.

Though all SU-100s look the same at a distance, there were more than 30 changes to the external appearance of SU-100s produced at UZTM in Sverdlovsk between September 1944 and March 1946. The small number of SU-100s produced at Plant №174 also featured changes in external appearance, and the majority of SU-100s produced by both plants were modernised post-war. The relatively rare service photographs also provided a

An SU-100 with tactical number 603, Vienna, April 1945. This early SU-100 was produced at UZTM before January 1945. The drive sprocket rollers are fixed with castellated nuts. There is no curved handrail on the sponson of commander's cupola, which appeared in December 1944 and remained a feature until the end of SU-100 production.

* *TsAMO - Central Archive of the Russian Ministry of Defence.*

chronology of improvements, but despite its relative "fame", the SU-100 is actually one of the rarest of Red Army armoured vehicles to have been photographed in wartime service.

The drawings provided in this book are based on the original plant design drawings and documentation, providing the precise angles of the hull armour plates, the methods of joining armour plates and the shape and dimensions of some relatively complex parts.

Long-held assumptions on the origins of some SU-100 components would appear to be erroneous. The SU-100 borrowed many parts from the T-34, but UZTM built complete T-34 tanks from October 1942 until as late as 1st March 1944, with distinct features specific to the plant. The plant did not however produce the later T-34-85 that was contemporary with the SU-100 in first line combat, and many of the parts used on the SU-100 built at UZTM were thereby a carry-over from the earlier UZTM produced T-34 chassis rather than the "contemporary" T-34-85. UZTM did not change the majority of its T-34 tooling and processes, so the SU-100 as produced until the last SU-100 was assembled in 1946 used some components from the 76.2mm F-34 armed T-34, which had long since been replaced in production by the T-34-85 at other

plants. Some parts were also indigenous to the Sverdlovsk plant, so there are design and production oddities, such as a slightly narrower (800x490mm) hatch on the armoured engine cover, while the same hatch produced for the T-34 at other plants - even starting with the early Kharkov produced T-34s - was 800x500mm. There were many such nuances, and the dimensions given are not an isolated production error on a single vehicle; the marginally narrower 490mm wide hatch was common to all SU-100s produced at UZTM.

It is not entirely appropriate to reference "series" or even "batches" of production with regard to the SU-100, as the SU-100 was modified on an ongoing basis throughout its short production life. Some modifications were undertaken to simplify production, to overcome component supply shortages or for eliminating defects to meet the requirements of military acceptance. The information available from the original production plant archives now however provides an accurate account of the chronological production history of the SU-100 on a month-by-month basis. By analysing the serial numbers of individual surviving SU-100s* all surviving examples can be traced to the month of original production, as detailed below:

Production Month and Year	Serial Numbers (original Cyrillic)	Production Number	Assembly Plant
September 1944	СУ409 XXX	40	UZTM, Sverdlovsk
October 1944	СУ410 XXX	90	UZTM, Sverdlovsk
November 1944	СУ411 XXX	150	UZTM, Sverdlovsk
December 1944	СУ412 XXX	220	UZTM, Sverdlovsk
January 1945	СУ412 XXX	210	UZTM, Sverdlovsk
February 1945	СУ412 XXX	215	UZTM, Sverdlovsk
March 1945	17 XXX	211	UZTM, Sverdlovsk
April 1945	47 XXXX	214	UZTM, Sverdlovsk
May 1945	8 XXXX	210	UZTM, Sverdlovsk
June 1945	58 XXX	210	UZTM, Sverdlovsk
July 1945	20 XXX	200	UZTM, Sverdlovsk
August 1945	71 XXX	200	UZTM, Sverdlovsk
September 1945	76 XXX	165	UZTM, Sverdlovsk
October 1945	83 XXX	160	UZTM, Sverdlovsk
November 1945	35 XXX	140	UZTM, Sverdlovsk
December 1945	57 XXX	150	UZTM, Sverdlovsk
January 1946	601Я XXXX	50	UZTM, Sverdlovsk
February 1946	602Я XXXX	100	UZTM, Sverdlovsk
March 1946	603Я XXXX	102	UZTM, Sverdlovsk
January 1947 - January 1948	701Г XXX, 702Г XXX, 703Г XXX etc. to 801Г XXX	204	Plant №174 Omsk

SU-100 serial numbers are located in the middle of the front hull nose beam, or at the top of the lower glacis plate on late type hulls without the cast beam used in construction.

«СУ», «Я» or «Г» - is the plant letter designation. Until 1945 UZTM production was coded with the letter "У" or "СУ" (self-propelled). In 1945 the serial number did not include a letter suffix, as both the plant and month of production were coded in the prefix. From 1946, UZTM in Sverdlovsk again used a letter designator, now "Я", while Plant №174 in Omsk used the prefix "Г". The number indicated by the "X" symbols in the table was the individual serial number of the SU-100 concerned, but starting from some designated point and not (as logic might dictate) from the beginning of the month, or year. Therefore, it is impossible to calculate precisely the number of SU-100s built in a given time period, but it can nevertheless be determined what SU-100 was produced earlier than another. It is generally believed, though to date not confirmed by documented proof, that these "XXX", "blocks" were stamped on the vehicles at the assembly stage in the plant, but the production month was stamped upon delivery and military acceptance. Because of other UZTM production commitments, an SU-100 might sometimes have clear features of production early in a given month, but with the serial number prefix of the next month (and sometimes even later). This would indicate that the given SU-100 had some defects requiring rework, and

the vehicle stood in the plant yard for quite some time before the defects were rectified and production completed. Such curiosities were however rare exceptions to the general rule.

September-December 1944

Production of both the SU-85M and the SU-100 began in September 1944 using the same chassis and casemate hull, with SU-85Ms being dispatched directly to front line units, but early production SU-100s being sent to training units and schools pending the arrival of sufficient quantities of 100mm anti-tank ammunition.

From the start of SU-85M and SU-100 series production in September 1944, these vehicles were fitted with extraction fans with the previously mentioned distinctive bell shaped cast armoured housing. In the document *"Temporary brief technical description of self-propelled artillery (unit) SU-85M"* dated August 1944 and approved by the plant Chief Engineer on 2nd September 1944 it was stated that: *"In comparison with (the) self-propelled SU-85 (the new) self-propelled housing has the following features: ...5. At the right rear corner of the roof are placed two armoured caps that protect the (ventilation) fans".*

The only difference between the series production SU-

SU-85Ms in Berlin, April 1945. The SU-85M used the hull and other components developed for the SU-100 for which delivery of the 100mm D-10S armament was delayed. Note the stamped early half-link tracks.

100 and the second prototype was the use of solid rubber tyres (rims) on the road wheels in place of the earlier type perforated with 42 holes. The change was made in accordance with design modifications made by the OKB of Plant №183 (which dictated the construction details for all Urals built T-34 tanks and related vehicles) several months previously, on 29th April 1944. In practice, road wheels with perforated solid tyres continued to be used on Uralmash built SU-85M and SU-100 SAUs until all available inventory was used up.

The early SU-100, as with the SU-85, SU-85M and both prototypes, used castellated nuts on the drive wheels. These were replaced by a piece of square section key steel, or 'splint' with a flat asymmetrical surface (described as asymmetric bonok in Russian), which became the standard retaining device for the drive wheel rollers from December 1944.

Series production SU-100s had four characteristic grooves on the right side of the cast gun mantlet. These were integrated into the casting to allow easier access for tightening the mantlet fastening bolts with a power tool during assembly. These grooves were more rounded and less distinct on early SU-100s.

Early production SU-100s produced in the autumn of 1944 featured a handrail for desant riders on the casemate side.

From January 1945 an additional handrail was welded directly to the sponson of the commander's cupola, and a shortened desant handrail mounted on the right side behind the sponson.

The tracks for both the SU-85M and the SU-100 were of the cast "waffle" type produced by workshop №110 within UZTM, or supplied by the affiliated Plant №50. The SU-100 also used the T-34 type stamped two-section half-links for the flat links without a guide horn.

Series production SU-100s used longer 5 metre tow cables (not including the thimble length) in place of the standard 4 metre cable used on the T-34, the SU-85 and both SU-100 prototypes. The reason was that it was impossible to couple the shorter tow cables to the front glacis tow hooks on the SU-100 as the casemate mounted gun barrel projected 3 metres ahead

Four threaded studs (for mounting a box to store a firewood heater) were welded to the rear armour plate on both prototypes and all series production SU-100s. SU-100s were delivered to Red Army units from UZTM with these stoves fitted from 1st October 1944 to 1st April 1945, however heating kits (stoves, blow lamps, petrol tanks for blow lamp fuel, heating mats) were not sent with SU deliveries during summer months, being separately despatched to warehouses.

The four grooves in the casting of the right side of the armoured gun mantlet were for convenience of locating the mounting bolts. The casting grooves had a smooth profile until February 1945.

From August 1945, the gun mantlet casting was changed, with modified mounting bolt grooves. This change was probably due to a change of foundry supplier, and not related to an engineering solution.

The gun mantlet as produced from February to July 1945 had more clearly defined mounting bolt grooves.

of the glacis, preventing a recovery vehicle from getting any closer. The 5 metre tow cables were usually mounted to the hull with one end attached to the right front tow hook and the cable stretched to a bracket under the rear right external fuel tank, to which the cable was attached by means of a belt. The second tow cable was attached to the right rear tow hook and pulled to a bracket welded on the left side of the fighting compartment track guard, where it was also fastened with a belt. Early production SU-100s had a bracket for the tow cable welded on the right front mudguard where it joined the side track guard, but it was not ever used for its intended purpose, this bracket having been a carry-over from the T-34 and SU-85, where it was used for attaching a shorter towing cable. On later SU-100s the bracket was moved to the left track guard.

The spares (ZIP) kit provided ex-works included 18 track grousers (located on the right track guard) and a large shovel mounted to the same track guard. A two-handed wood saw was mounted on the left side of the casemate, and the folded tarpaulin was stowed near the left external fuel tanks. Tow cable shackles were located at the rear of the left track guard with the traditional T-34 type ZIP boxes. The mechanical spares ZIP

box was located on the right track guard, with the ZIP box for the armament located on the left track guard. Spare track links were bolted to the SU-100 glacis plate at the plant, but with seven links rather than four as with the T-34 tank, a practice carried over from the SU-85 to increase frontal armour protection. As spare track links were now bolted to the glacis, the "spares and repair" track set supplied by the production plant was reduced from 230 track links of each type to 210 track links without guide horns and 190 tracks with guide horns. There were dissenters within USA GBTU on this seemingly benign issue, and a defined agreement between the plant and rear services was reached only in February 1945.

The SU-100 featured a small hatch in the right corner of the front lower armoured plate, as on the SU-85. Its purpose was to access the nut for parting the crank drive wheel, thereby allowing adjustment of the starboard track tension. A similar nut crank port drive wheel was accessed internally from the driver-mechanic's compartment - as in the T-34 - but the right side of the SU-100 fighting compartment was occupied by eight artillery rounds, so turning the crank was only possible from the outside through the hatch opening. Undertaking this operation with a wrench while lying on the (at best - dry) ground was a dirty, awkward and uncomfortable procedure, and was therefore generally avoided by the crew, which is the reason why the right track on SU-100s was often observed as being slack…

The tracks were tightened by turning the crank on each side with a special key through small apertures in the upper front armour plate which were protected by armoured plugs, as on the T-34 tank. After removing the plugs, a crank was then fixed in position and the gear ring engaged with its counterpart on the hull. It was possible to hit the guide wheel with a sledgehammer, but to do so was strictly prohibited so as to prevent the destruction of the hub bearings. A special tightening crank was located in the ZIP set provided for each vehicle. To reconnect the crank

The later type of external fuel tank fastening, with steel bands bolted directly to the mounting brackets, was used on SU-100 production from 1st January 1945 until production ceased in 1948.

The early type of external fuel tank fastening, using steel bands with tightening bolts located in the middle of the bands, were used on SU-85 and SU-100 production until 1st January 1945.

Early type MDSh mounting brackets were removed from service SU-100s during post-war modernization, and are today seen only on museum exhibits which were decommissioned before modernisation.

The mountings for the BDSh-5 (Bolshaya Dymovaya Shashka - large smoke barrel, smoke generation time - 5 minutes) cannister-type smoke generators were unified with those mounted on the rear of the T-34-85.

The BDSh-5 smoke cannister mounting (here seen on a T-34-85, but the SU-100 mounting was identical).

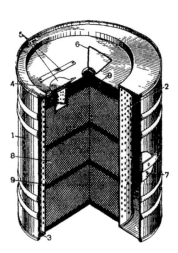

Рис. 54. Дымовая шашка БДШ-5:
1 — наружный цилиндр; 2 — внутренний сетчатый цилиндр; 3 — днище, 4 — крышка; 5 — запальное устройство; 6 — ручка; 7 — клапан дымовыходного отверстия,

The BDSh-5 smoke cannister.

This T-34 tank is equipped with early type MDSh smoke cannisters.

drive wheel gears, a fixture was attached to a tow hook, its cable was passed through an access window in the track guard, and by turning the key with ratchet the track along with the guide wheel was tightened to the hull. The front track guards on the SU-100 produced by UZTM until the end of the production were of the rounded type (taken directly from the T-34) and did not fold back on hinges, hence the horizontal access windows with dirt guard covers were installed in the vertical walls of the track guards to allow the crank cable to be passed through. On later SU-100s the design was changed, with strips being welded to the front armoured plate to engage the crank.

Only a small number of SU-100s were produced in September and October 1944, and these were sent to military schools in the rear rather than to combat units at the front. The delayed delivery of SU-100s to the front when the SU-100 chassis was in production was as stated entirely down to problems with 100mm ammunition availability. The 100mm D-10S gun was developed on the basis of the calibre of the 100mm M-1940 (B-34) naval universal gun, as used on "Project 26" Kirov class light cruisers, which was designed for firing at naval surface and air targets. To develop a new gun and begin series production of hundreds of units rather than the smaller number required for naval installations was not in of itself a major problem, but the availability of the correct ammunition types in large quantities was very much a difficulty. Ammunition for naval guns was of course available and already in production, but was specific, being HE and utilising time-delay fuses. There was no armour piercing round available when the SU-100 was originally envisioned. The new SU-100 could not

The later type BDSh-5 smoke canister, mounted on a T-34-85 tank.

thereby be sent to the front to combat new German tank types while it lacked suitable ammunition to do so. Production of the 100mm armour-piercing 53-UBR-412 APHE round and the 53-BR-412 round with an armour-piercing-tracer arrowhead projectile had just begun as the SU-100 was being readied for series production, so combat units began to receive this ammunition only in October-November. Accordingly, formation of the first SU-100 armed self-propelled artillery regiments began in November 1944, with earlier produced SU-100s having in the interim been sent to training schools, a "luxury" the Red Army by 1944 could afford.

February 1945

In February 1945, new hull construction drawings were issued, with design changes again concentrating on the elimination of cracks in the armour at the corners of cut sections. The first batch of seven experimental hulls with a modified fighting compartment design was welded together in February. The main visible change was the elimination of the vertical section of the loader's hatch in the rear armour plate of the fighting compartment.

In February 1945, a modified foundry casting master mould was made for the gun mantlet castings, such that from February production the grooves on the right of the cast gun mantlet over the heads of the mounting bolts became sharper and more distinct, this casting mould pattern remaining in use until the end of July 1945.

Despite the new armament, the SU-85 and SU-100 used the same 1260x200x200mm armament ZIP set box as the

The upper and lower frontal hull armour plates on the early SU-100 were welded to a cast beam. Note the additional armour on the gun mantlet.

76.2mm F-34 armed T-34 tank. It was however originally mounted on the left track guard closer to the front of the SU-100, but was later moved further to the rear, in the period January-February 1945.

March 1945

Mass production of modified SU-100 fighting compartment as described above began in mid-March, with the SU-100 from this time onward also having no vertical rear section to the loader's hatch. Another small change that occurred in March was that the cast letter "P." (in Russian "R") disappeared from the driver-mechanic's hatch cover. Interestingly, the driver-mechanic's hatch cover on the SU-85 self-propelled gun was adorned with a letter "C." (in Russian "S") including the full stop, meaning "самоход" (self-propelled). Documents defining the official meaning of these letters have not to date been uncovered, but the design logic can be understood. UZTM cast armoured parts for many different military vehicles, including for supply to other plants. The driver-mechanic's hatch cover on the SU-122 was much narrower than the T-34 driver-mechanic's hatch so there could be no mistaking it for a standard T-34 hatch. But the hatch cover for the SU-85 was externally very similar to that for the T-34, differing only in detail, hence marked with the Russian letter "C." for "самоход" as noted in plant documents of the 1940s). In turn, on the new hatch cover for SU-100 self-propelled gun the thickness of the frontal armour plate was increased to 75mm to match the glacis armour. It outwardly remained similar in detail to the hatch used for the earlier SU-85, but when UZTM terminated T-34 tank and SU-85 SPG hatch cover production, the SU-100 hatch no longer required any special markings to distinguish it, however the letter "P" (Russian - "равнопрочный" - i.e. "same strength as

The upper and lower frontal hull armour plates on the late SU-100, as produced from May 1945, were directly welded without a cast beam.

The early type mortice jointed glacis armour as produced until May 1945. Note the shape of the armour plate.

The early type mortice jointed lower frontal armour hull plate as produced until May 1945.

The later and simplified lower frontal armour hull plate.

the front armour plate") disappeared only when a new casting mould master pattern was made.

In relation to the SU-100 driver-mechanic's hatch the term "равнопрочный " was used in the manuscript *A brief technical description of the prototype model*" * which was effective at UZTM from June 1944, which also deciphers the origins of the mysterious letter "P." on the casting. From 15th March 1945, SU-100s were also provided with a TSh-19 (heated) gun sight.

April 1945

According to the "Order to structure changes of the Chief Designer UZTM №58" dated from 1st April, SU-100s were now to be provided 6.5 metre length tow cables ex-works, in agreement with the content of correspondence between the acting district engineer USA GBTU KA Engineer-Lieutenant Colonel Agrikov and the head of the Red Army USA GBTU Major-General engineering tank service Alymov**. The reason for again extending the length of the tow cables was as before related to locating the cable on the front tow hooks of a self-propelled gun with a long barrel but obviously no turret allowing the gun to be rotated out of the way to the rear. Correspondence about

the need to extend the towing ropes had been ongoing since from January 1945.

New tow cable fixing procedures were also determined: The cable thimble of one tow cable was now attached to the left front tow hook and dragged to a bracket on the right side under the rear reserve fuel tank (nothing prevented the other tow hook and opposite bracket being used - post war was this was normally done). The second tow cable end was located on the left rear tow hook and dragged to a bracket on the left front track guard (moved from the right side).

Early SU-100s were fitted with the 9-RM radio station. According to the *"Order to structure changes of the Chief Designer UZTM №52"* dated 20th March 1945, the improved 9-RS ("Tur") radio station was now specified, this being installed on production vehicles starting from 15th April.

The 9-RM ("Tapir-M") radio set was manufactured from April 1943 by Plant №203 in the name of Ordzhonikidze which had been evacuated from Moscow to the city of Sarapul. The RSI-4T "Malyutka" (little one) receiver sets was built by Plant №590, the "Electrosignal" plant, which had been evacuated from Voronezh to Novosibirsk in Siberia. In 1944, Plant

* TsAMO Fund 38, Inventory 11369, Case 460.   ** TsAMO, Fund 38 Inventory 11369 Case 507.

The early type mortice jointed rear fighting compartment armour plate welding as produced until January 1945. Note the cracks in the armour near the mortice joints. The armour profile was modified to eliminate these stress points.

№203 began production of the improved 9 RS "Tur" radio set with markedly better performance, and began to supply it to tank plants instead of the 9-RM. As the new 9-RM radio set was the same size and no alterations were required to install it, the military representative at UZTM allowed its installation in the SU-100 - for which he received an official reprimand. Despite the radio being more effective, the military representative at UZTM had no authority to make such a change, which was strictly speaking a decision to be taken by a testing commission after trials with a new radio set fitted in an SU-100 for trials. The trial was thereby duly held post-factum, the logical approval of the new radio installation was recorded in the official minutes, and the new radio set legally "registered" as the standard fitting for the SU-100, so as to indicate that all procedures had been adhered to.

May 1945

Multiple design changes were undertaken on the SU-100 during May 1945. The war was effectively over by the first days of the month, and design time was thereby allocated to increasing durability and eliminating known defects that had not directly affected fighting capability, but which had been ignored while the priority had remained maximising wartime production output.

In particular the casemate hull of the SU-100 was signi-

The intermediate type rear fighting compartment armour plate layout as produced from January 1945 to May 1945.

The late type rear fighting compartment armour, much simplified without the use of triangular gussets, as produced from May 1945. The modification was again to eliminate armour cracking in the welded trianglular gussets.

ficantly modified. According to an *"Order to structure changes of the Chief Designer UZTM"*, from 1st May 1945 the SU-100 was to be built with a "beamless hull", i.e. the upper and lower frontal armoured plates were now to be directly butt-welded. There was not however an immediate change in production, as UZTM took some time to convert production while using up existing inventory of cut and prepared armour sections.

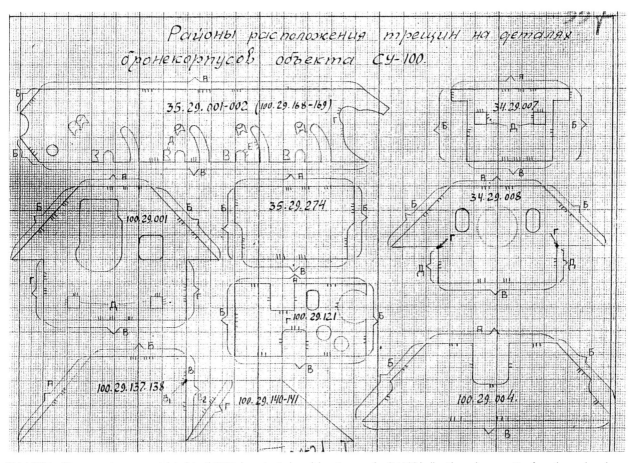

This UZTM military acceptance report dated April 1945 shows typical crack locations on the SU-100 hull, with cracks emanating from the angles where armour plates have been cut. All changes to the hull armour fabrication layout were made in order to eliminate this stress cracking.

All SU-100s with casemate hulls on which assembly had begun prior to 1st May - i.e. with the frontal armour plates welded to a cast beam - were delivered to the Red Army during May 1945. There are therefore some preserved SU-100s today with May production serial numbers but still featuring a frontal cast beam glacis construction. Two examples are SU-100 №81388 located at the "Prokhorovka Field Battle Museum" - commissioned in May SU-100 with the "April fighting compartment" and SU-100 №81458 at the "Museum of T-34 Tank" located in the village of Sholokhovo to the north east of Moscow.

The modified SU-100 glacis using directly joined frontal armour plates was 100mm longer than the earlier cast beam type, therefore the location mounting points for the spare track links on the glacis were lowered slightly on the glacis plate. The SU-85 pattern rounded and non-folding track guards were retained however. Although the box section folding type front track guard had been modified on T-34-85 assembly drawings made by Plant №183 from October 1944, these box section guards were not introduced on the SU-100 until near the end

of SU-100 post-war production. All wartime SU-100s thereby had rounded front track guards.

From May 1945 the welded triangular gusset plate between the rear wall of the fighting compartment and the engine compartment (MTO) was eliminated on all SU-100 production, as it had proven a source of armour cracking as a result of welding several sections of pre-hardened armour together at stress points.

In May 1945, the lower frontal plate armour thickness was increased from 45 to 60mm. The rectangular straps for the late-type front idler meshing device mounting began to be welded to the glacis plate, and the slots with blanking plates for passing the wire of the device through the front track guard side were moved forward to align with the welded straps straps. Early May production SU-100s with casemate hulls featuring a cast front beam as assembled in April had the straps welded to the junction of this beam with the glacis plate, directly on top of the weld. Some surviving museum examples have the strap shifted closer to the nose or located on the front cast

33

The early type of armoured housing (for the internal detent clamp) above the gun recoil system on the fighting compartment roof. Two circular gudgeons are located at opposite ends of the armoured copola. (V. Shaikin)

The late type of armoured housing detent clamp above the gun recoil system. The two circular gudgeons are in parallel at the rear of the housing.

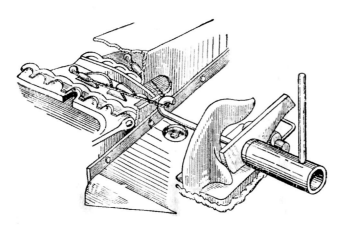

Рис. 231. Введение в зацепление зубьев кривошипа приспособлением

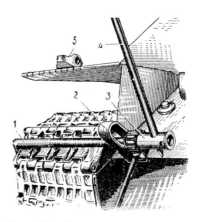

Рис. 153. Введение в зацепление кривошипа механизма натяжения при помощи приспособления:
1 — стяжной крюк; 2 — упор; 3 — специальная гайка; 4 — лом; 5 — захват

The early type track adjustment device, which located the meshing ring gear of the front idler with that fixed to the idler spigot mounting on the hull. This device was attached to the tow hook.

The late type of track adjustment device. This device was attached to the special rectangular strip welded to the hull glacis armour.

beam of the earlier production casemate hulls. Their location was changed slightly on subsequent upgrades when all SU-100 were fitted with box construction front mudguards. In early June 1945 production, the small hatch for gaining access the nut retainer crank for tensioning the right track was slightly recessed, but by the end of the month a new hatches was used in production, now again level with the (now 60mm) lower frontal armour plate.

The first early May production casemate fighting compartments featured a modified panorama telescope sight hatch cover and loader's hatch cover. The loader's hatch was modified, now with four section hinges rather than six. The latch for fixing the cover in the open position remained on the right hinge, but the stop limit with its rubber damper was moved to the left

hatch cover. There was also a change in the size of the panoramic telescope hatch covers, which on early production SU-100s had been the same as for the SU-85. The hatch with its panoramic sight was increased in size from 600x580mm to 670x650 mm (the hinge mountings of the larger hatch cover no longer fitted between the hatch and the armoured cupola under the gun detent system, so a cut-out was provided). The Mk.4 on the left side of the old panoramic sight hatch was not fitted.

The loader's hatch cover was increased in size from 700x500mm to 760x570mm, the design of the hatches being changed to prevent water ingress into the crew compartment. The early fighting compartment roof hatch covers were flush with the fighting compartment roof, and leaked badly during rainy weather. The new hatch designs included coamings that

The SU-85 type oval blanking cover on the side of the front track guard allowed for passage of the cable for the early type track adjustment device.

Both SU-100 prototypes and series production SU-100s used SU-85 type track guards with oval blanking covers until May 1945.

The rectangular strips for the late-type track adjuster were welded into position from May 1945. The blanking covers were moved forward and now located vertically.

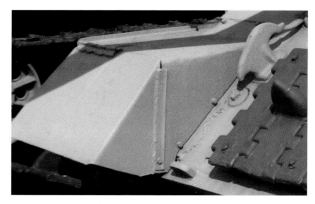

SU-100s were provided with a new angular construction and hinged track guard from the start of SU-100 production at Plant №174 in Omsk in 1947. This type of track guard was earlier produced in Omsk for the T-34-85 tank. The strips for the track adjustment device mounting were now welded closer to the bow, reducing interference with the spare track links bolted to the glacis. As the track guards were now hinged they could be moved out of the way, eliminating the need for an access window. From 1947, all SU-100s were gradually modified with these new track guards during capital repair, with the Plant №174 track guard arrangement being adopted on all service SU-100s. On early SU-100s the mounting was welded to the cast nose beam.

By contrast with the SU-100, early T-34-85 tanks featured oval apertures in the track guards for the track adjustment device, but without blanking covers.

SU-100s produced until March 1945 featured a loader's hatch with a small, hinged section located in the rear armour plate

The vertical folding section of the loader's hatch in the rear armour plate was deleted from March 1945, partly to simplify assembly, but primarily in order to eliminate stress cracks.

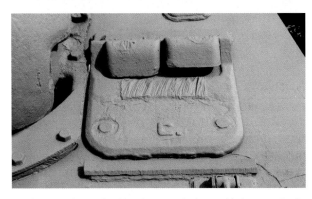

The driver-mechanic's hatch on the SU-85 had a moulded Russian Cyrillic letter "S" letter (meaning "samokhod" - self propelled gun) to distinguish it from similar hatch covers produced at UZTM for series production T-34 tanks.

The mounting bracket for the tow cables was later moved to the rear of the left track guard. (A. Buylov)

Left: The ZIP box for the main armament was moved slightly further to the rear of SU-100s produced from January-February 1945.

Early SU-100 driver-mechanic's hatches had the moulded Russian Cyrillic letter "R" (meaning ravnoprochnaya - increased thickness to 75mm and modified armour plate), again to distinguish it from similar hatch covers produced for T-34 tanks at UZTM until March 1945.

The late SU-100 driver-mechanic's hatch cover was reconfigured, the original mould form having been milled to improve the overall appearance, albeit the finish remained rough. This form was introduced in November 1945.

The stud mounting for attaching the tow cable location brackets on later SU-100s. (A. Buylov)

overlapped the hatch openings, now with rubber gaskets and tin flanging around the perimeter of the roof hatch openings, somewhat improving crew comfort in inclement weather.

In May, a known engineering defect was resolved. The increased frontal armour of the SU-100 as compared with the SU-85 had caused early SU-100s to suffer suspension overloading and premature destruction of the front road wheels in operational use. The front left and two front right wheel stations were particularly affected because the gun was offset from the longitudinal axis. Overloading of the front wheels led to rapid deterioration of the wheel discs, the solid rubber tyres (rims) and the ball bearing hubs. Alternative solutions were tested in March, with a new hub on three bearings, and with a thicker wheel disk and old type wheel, but also with the hub on three bearings.

With effect from the hundredth SU-100 produced at UZTM in May 1945, the original two bearing stub axle construction was replaced with a three bearing construction. At the same time the road wheels were now stamped from 16mm sheet steel rather than 10mm, with the smaller 16mm wheel disks studs and bolts now increased to 20mm diameter. The outer ring of bolts that attached the wheel disc to the hub was increased to 30mm on the front wheel station, remaining 24mm on the other wheel stations.

At the end of May the first twelve SU-100s were produced armed with a modified gun, a single, vertical axis stabilised 100mm D-10SK (SK-"самокомпенсированная" - self compensated). The gun is sometimes (and erroneously) referred

to as the D-10СУ ("самоуравновешенная" - self balanced), apparently as the original GAU index for the D-10S was 52-PS-412 and thereby the D-10SK might logically be the GAU index 52-PS-412У. However, contemporary documents refer to the gun only to the D-10SK.

SU-100s armed with the later 100mm D-10SK gun are recognised by the reinforced tapered trunk of the gun barrel as it is mounted into the gun mantlet, replacing the uniform cylindrical barrel of the early D-10S gun barrel. Many earlier production SU-100s were later re-armed with the 100mm D-10SK in the post-war decades during capital rebuilds. Some SU-100s released to museums before capital rebuild retained the original armament however. Examples include the SU-100 number СУ412775 at the Kubinka Tank Museum, which is in running order, and an SU-100 mounted on a plinth at the "Prokhorovka Battlefield" museum reserve.

In addition to improving gun targeting and aim when on the move, balancing the gun also reduced wear on the vertical aiming flywheel and increased the overall durability of all the moving parts of the gun aiming system. Both producers of the D-10S gun in Sverdlovsk, i.e. Plant №8, and №9, had developed their own solutions and prototypes for the modernised gun; however as was common in Soviet development, it was a third prototype, combining the best features of both rival designs, that would become the production 100mm D-10SK gun.

The GAU and GBU testing commission approved the D-10SK gun for series production in April*. The additional weight of the new D-10SK gun was balanced by reducing the

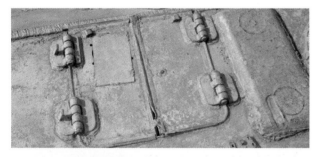

The panoramic sight hatch as produced to May 1945. The front left hatch hinge is clipped to accommodate the flange of the MK. 4 periscope. The metal stops next to the left side hinges are to prevent hitting the periscope housing on the fighting compartment roof. (V. Shaikin and A. Lagutin)

The late type panoramic sight hatch as produced from May 1945. The hatch is modified, now slightly wider and with the right side hinges clipped, also opening was made easier due to additional torsion assistance.

*TsAMO, Fund 38, Inventory 11369, Case 529

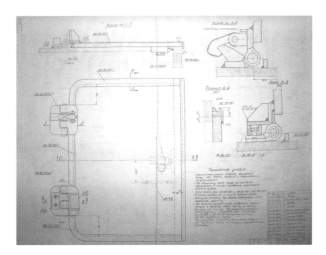

A plant drawing from May 1945 showing the late type loader's hatch cover with new type of hatch locking mechanism which was introduced from November 1945.

The early type loader's hatch cover as produced until May 1945. Note the six section hinge, open position locking mechanism and stop limit on the right hinge, and the narrow hatch surround.

The late type loader's hatch cover as produced from May 1945. Note the four section hinge, the stop limit now with rubber damper moved to the left hinge, and the hatch surround is wide and flat. This type of lock was designed in November 1945.

thickness of the gun barrel compared with the D-10S, and so to compensate for any reduction in gun barrel integrity, the barrel was strengthened at the point of maximum combusted gas pressure as the gun fired. The step or "ledge" at the base of the earlier cylindrical D-10S barrel was replaced with a barrel design featuring a smooth tapered transition near the base. The change added 64kg to the weight of the barrel, directly above the already strained front road wheels and suspension mountings, hence the simultaneous modifications to the front suspension. The electric trigger on the D-10SK was also updated to the new RT-9 type. All new SU-100s produced from June 1945 were armed with the modified D-10SK gun with the conical trunk of the new gun being the primary external distinguishing feature of the SU-100 armed with its standard "post-war" D-10SK armament.

There were other detail changes undertaken in May 1945, such as the distance between the vertical crosspieces on the side grilles of the engine compartment being changed slightly.

June 1945

All SU-100 built in June 1945 were armed with the modified D-10SK gun. The engine compartment deck handrails were moved from the rear towards the middle of the side covers. During later modernisation in the 1960s they were moved again on some SU-100s, in order to make room for attaching MDSh-5 smoke canisters.

From 1st June by "Order to structure changes" №137 from the office of the Chief Designer (OGK) at UZTM, a new container was approved for crew personal belongings to be mounted on the front starboard track shoulder*. This early container design proved unsuccessful however, as it was easily damaged by undergrowth. It is not clearly documented whether SU-100s produced from June to November were equipped these first generation crew stowage containers, but a modified container was introduced on production SU-100s from November. Post-war SU-100 crews were being provided with ergonomic and social "luxuries" unheard of during the war.

July 1945

From July the second handrail behind the commander's turret sponson on the right side of the fighting compartment casemate was deleted, there now being only a handrail welded onto the sponson. Self-extraction equipment also began to be fitted on the left side of the fighting compartment from July 1945, consisting of two loops of steel cable, with the ends terminated in a block for fastening to the track links through the bolt-holes

---

*Letter dated 31st May 1945 TSAMO, Fund 38, Inventory 11369, Case 507

in the links used for mounting the removable grousers. Using two such loops, a log was tied to the tracks, forward movement dragging the log under the SU-100, with the aim of extracting the vehicle.

August 1945

Deep grooves were made on the right side of the fixed section of the gun mantlet casting, designed to facilitate access to the heads of mounting bolts, with the grooves becoming smooth again due to a change of the foundry master in August.

Also in August, the loader's hatch and engine deck locks were changed. There are however often different combinations of old and new locks from vehicle to vehicle.

September 1945

In September 1945, changes were made to the design of the commander's cupola, again to prevent water ingress. There was no change in outward appearance, but rubber sealing gaskets were now fitted (in particular, under the flange of the Mk.4 periscope viewing device) and plans were in September submitted for a modified, enlarged commander's cupola with a single hatch, which would later enter production.

The V-2 engine used in the SU-100 and T-34-85 had significant oil consumption. This was accepted from an oil consumption viewpoint, but the problem was from an operational standpoint formally addressed in September 1945, from which date plant documents showed that one of the 90

Compare the flush hatch coamings of the early type loader's hatch (top) with the new type loader's hatch (below). (A. Buylov)

The leading wheel pairs were strengthened in May 1945. The modified front wheels were stamped from 16mm sheet steel rather than 10mm as used as standard, and fitted with larger 20mm diameter studs and nuts on the outer circle - the second to fifth roadwheel pairs retained the use of standard 16mm studs and nuts.

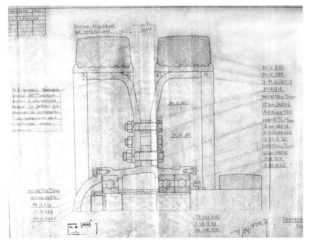

An Uralmashzavod Plant drawing detailing the strengthened of the front road wheels, using 16mm sheet steel stampings and 20mm studs and nuts.

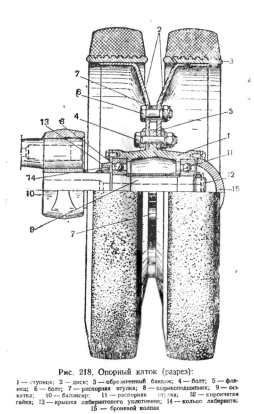

Рис. 218. Опорный каток (разрез):
1 — ступица; 2 — диск; 3 — обрезиненный бандаж; 4 — болт; 5 — флянец; 6 — болт; 7 — распорная втулка; 8 — шарикоподшипник; 9 — ось катка; 10 — балансир; 11 — распорная втулка; 12 — коронцатая гайка; 13 — крышка лабиринтового уплотнения; 14 — кольцо лабиринта; 15 — броневой колпак

Drawing from a contemporary manual of the strengthened front wheels. All bolts are now of the same 20mm diameter, with three hub bearings rather than two hub bearings as used on the early wheel type.

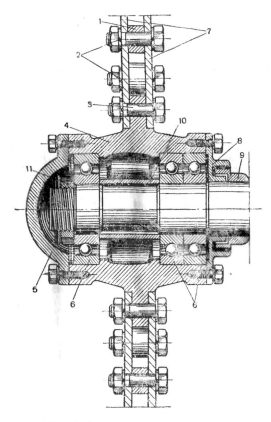

Рис. 219. Крепление переднего опорного катка:
1 — проставочные втулки; 2 — стяжные болты; 3 — болты крепления дисков; 4 — ступица катка; 5 — броневой колпак; 6 — шариковые подшипники катка; 7 — диски опорного катка; 8 — крышка лабиринтового уплотнения; 9 — кольцо лабиринтового уплотнения; 10 — распорная втулка; 11 — коронцатая гайка

litre reserve fuel tanks should be used for lubricating oil rather than diesel fuel. Much later the left rear reserve tank was (on both the SU-100 and T-34-85) marked "масло" (oil), though the remaining three reserve tanks were not always marked "топливо" (fuel). BTiMV KA Order №243 dated 6th September 1945, which was formally issued to the plant by the district inspector and senior military representative of the Red Army USA GBTU* on 10th September 1945 instructed the plant on the specifics of shipping new SU-100s:

"All assemblies and mechanisms are to be filled with winter grades of grease. After loading the (rail) cars on the (railway) platform, the oil is to be drained from the oil lubrication system and the oil tanks. A single refill of oil for the diesel (engine) lubrication system is to be sent with the echelon (convoy). Lubricating oil should be contained in one of the reserve fuel tanks, and marked "oil".

How often mistakes were made with filling the reserve tanks in practice is unrecorded; however as the reserve tanks were not plumbed into the engine fuel or lubrication systems, any mistake in filling the tanks would not be critical as any error would be caught before use.

October 1945

In October 1945, the first SU-100s with the enlarged commander's cupola with a single hatch, as introduced on the T-34-85 from January 1945 and designed for the SU-100 in September, were completed, with full series production of this type being from November 1945. The first 30 SU-100s with a new torsion spring for the loader's hatch - now mounted externally rather than internally were also produced in October. The new design was recommended for use on all SU-100 production, but the change was widely introduced only in December. The desant handrails mounted on the engine deck were now welded in place almost centrally on the side engine covers on all SU-100s rather than further towards the rear as before. The fuel filler for the front fuel tanks was modified for easing the process of fuelling the front internal fuel tanks, with the armoured plug being increased in diameter from 90 to 120mm. Finally, sprung latches were added to the tow hooks.

November 1945

The most noticeable change on SU-100s produced from November 1945 was the general introduction on all SU-100s of

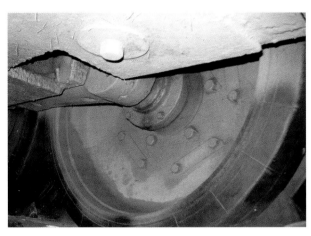

The road wheel inner surface. Note the locking nut strips - common to all UZTM SPG production. These strips were introduced in the summer of 1943 (15th July 1943) at Plant Nº183, and also later at UZTM). The fuel tank drain plug is evident in the foreground. Post-war, feedback from the Red (Soviet) Army requested UZTM to modify the protruding plug which was occasionally damaged by rocks, but the design was not changed before SU-100 production ceased.

Early SU-85 type rubber rims with 42 perforations were used on both SU-100 prototypes. There is no inscription on the rims.

Production of rims with 42 perforations was curtailed on 29th April 1944. However the same mould was modified by filling the cores for production of the solid rims, leaving the imprint of the perforations of the earlier rim type in evidence. Interestingly, these rims were produced in the 1950s, with rim dimensions 830x150x660 stamped into the metal mould used to form the rims.

Another variant of the imprinted rim dimensions, again based on the old mould with blanked off holes. This rim was produced in April 1950 for the T-44M. (A. Aksenov)

The most common rim variant of the rim as used on the final production SU-100s assembled at UZTM in the autumn of 1945. These rims were produced by several plants, and into the 1960s. After SU-100 production ceased, SU-100s underwent capital repair also using wheels from the T-34-85 and T-44 in addition to spares produced for the SU-100.

Left: The 634mm drive sprocket with castellated nuts on the roller bearings. Centre: The same drive sprocket type with roller bearing caps as used on the SU-100 from late 1944 until production ceased. Right: The 650mm diameter drive sprocket diameter was developed at Plant №183 in March 1945 and is easily recognized by the small service holes. Such drive sprockets were installed on the SU-100 during post-war capital rebuilds.

the enlarged commander's sponson and cupola with the single "shovel" type single hatch, which would after November remained unchanged until the end of SU-100 production. The armour thickness on this commander's sponson and cupola was, as with its predecessor, not uniform, being up to 90mm at the front and 60-75mm around the circumference. When viewed from above, the sponson was elliptical rather than round in shape. Due to the larger diameter of the new cupola and hatch, the distinctive 20mm ledge between the sponson and the cupola edge on the outer side of the sponson evident on earlier production SU-100s disappeared.

An "order of changes" from the OGK (the chief design office) at UZTM dated 8th October 1945 established improvements in the design of the (original but unsuccessful) stowage container for crew personal belongings on the right track guard. From 15th November, all newly manufactured SU-100s featured stowage containers with strengthening ribs in the sheet metal pressings, a modified internal shelf and external locks with solid rather than spot welding.

In another rare post-war "cosmetic" improvement, the driver-mechanic's hatch was now machined before installation rather than left with rough casting marks, such that the appearance of the hatch became smoother.

At the end of November 1945 the shape of the "trough" above the engine compartment around the raised engine access hatch housing was modified and moved 90mm to the rear. The new "short-trough" (a descriptive term used for explanation, and not found in any documents) had a horizontal area in front of the hatch with a length of about 70mm, rather than 95mm on the early "long-trough" type cover. Though a minor dimensional change, the overall proportions of the engine deck were modified as a result, hence identifying later SU-100s as post November 1945 production. The "short-trough" modification was used on all subsequent SU-100s until the end of production in 1948 at Plant №174 in Omsk.

A new lock type for the loader's hatch and the engine compartment roof hatches was approved in August, and these were installed in November with a view to introducing the

The SU-100 with 100mm D-10S gun installation, with an abrupt transition between gun barrel and gun mantlet. (E. Golovashkin)

The later SU-100, as armed with the modified D-10SK gun. Installed from June 1945, and thereby a post- (European) war modification, the D-10SK gun installation has a smooth tapered strengthening "collar" between the barrel and the gun mantlet. (A. Buylov)

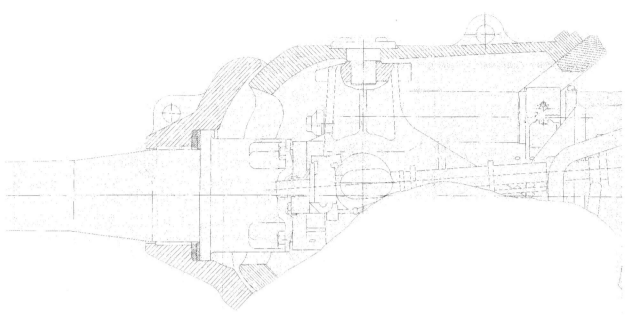

Drawing of the later 100mm D-10SK gun with its distinctive tapered barrel base.

This photograph of two SU-100s parked up before the 75th anniversary Victory Parade in Moscow in 2020 shows the detail differences between vehicles. The SU-100 in the foreground was armed (or late re-armed) with a 100mm D-10SK gun with the fluted base to the barrel. The SU-100 in the immediate background is armed with a wartime production 100mm D-10S gun. (Andrey Aksenov)

The distinctive post-war stowage box for crew personal kit was introduced in November 1945.

Although the later, and standard post-war crew personal effects stowage box was sturdier than the original design, the sheet steel container remained fragile as damage evident on service photographs clearly shows.

The handrails were moved to a new central position on the engine compartment side covers from June 1945.

The self-extrication cable and its mounting on the left side of the fighting compartment side was introduced in July 1945.

The early type engine compartment hatch and lock. (E. Golovashkin)

Left: The handrails for desant infantry use were located at the rear of the engine compartment side covers on early production SU-100s.

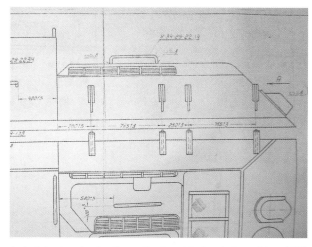

A plant drawing showing the positioning of the handrails as of June 1945.

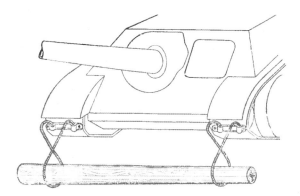

Рис. 280. Способ крепления бревна к гусеницам при самовытаскивании

A drawing from a Soviet manual showing the methodology for using the self-extrication equipment.

The later type engine compartment hatch and lock as produced from August 1945. (A. Buylov)

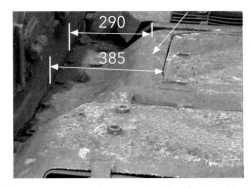

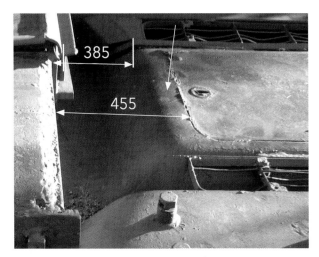

The early type of convex engine compartment roof section. The convex form was changed at the end of November 1945. The early version had a longer horizontal area in front of the hatch, and the hatch was located closer to the rear of the fighting compartment (385mm - early version, 455mm - later version). (A. Buylov)

The late type engine compartment convex roof section.

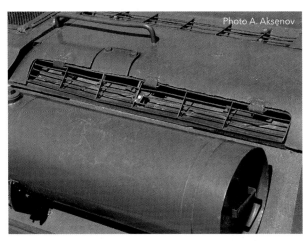

There were many detail changes between early and late production SU-100s. Note here the changing profile of the air grille mountings: the early type grill (left), and the new type grill introduced from May 1945 (right).

change on all SU-100s in December after minor fettling. In practice, the new locks were often used on the loaders hatch but the old type lock kept on the hatch over the engine.

December 1945 - March 1946

After the end of the war, the Red Army made requests to equip the driver-mechanic's hatch with transparent visors to improve the driver-mechanic's lot. With the hatch open, the driver-mechanic of the SU-100, as with the T-34, sat in the airflow sucked through the fan motor hatch at the rear of the fighting compartment (the bulkhead between the fighting and engine compartments not being airtight, and the fan being powerful). In rainy weather sprayed dirt and water compounded the misery for the driver-mechanic. In December 1945, experimental canvas shrouds were designed for the driver-mechanic's hatch, to prevent rainwater leakage through the hatch hinge. The covers were installed on four SU-100s for trials purposes. None

of the planned improvements were introduced however, so the construction remained unchanged until SU-100 production ceased at UZTM in March 1946, incorporating only the improvements introduced in November.

By the end of 1945, major changes were underway as the Soviet Union rapidly adjusted to a post-war civilian economy and defence manufacturing was restructured. UZTM began to redirect engineering development towards the production of oilfield equipment, while a shortage of specialist workers began to affect production. The reduction in military orders had resulted in less production, and less income for the workers, who had began to resign due to the reduction in salaries. The Uralmash plant also produced parts for the IS-2 and IS-3 heavy tanks and the ISU-152, and was thereby not entirely focused on the SU-100 in the immediate post-war era. The head of USA GBTU of Red Army, General-Major Engineering Tank Service Nikolai Nikolaievich Alimov accordingly on 3rd

December 1945 sent a memorandum to Deputy People's Commissar of Heavy Machine Building (NKTP) of the USSR Yakov V. Yushin:

"A very difficult situation has formed with the implementation of the SU-100 Self-Propelled Artillery (piece) production programme at Uralmashzavod. Assembly and delivery of (the) SAU in the month of November this year was extremely spasmodic, the result in addition to the threat of failure of the SAU production programme (being the) possible and lowering of their quality, especially at the end of the month. The demobilisation attitudes have appeared related to SU-100 production, both from the management of the plant and in the workshops and departments, with significantly lower attention to the quality of combat vehicles for the Red Army".

The district engineer of USA GBTU, Red Army Engineer-Colonel Zukher in his report to N. N. Alymov dated 22nd November 1945, described the situation in the manufacturing plant in more detail:

"The Announcement at the plant about the end of production of the SU-100 and the demobilisation of workers in the shops and departments of the plant, as evidenced by the failure to introduce changes in the orders of the Chief-Designer Department, as well as a shortage of parts, assemblies....(has led to) qualified tank assembly personnel and test-mechanics being redistributed for other work. So, for example, in the control and acceptance workshop, only five experienced drivers remained... the failure of the production plan in workshop №190 is due to the following reasons: For the last 2-3 months, 170 workers from the total available workforce of 600 have left the workshop. In October, the workshop worked primarily on civil drilling machines and Uralmashzavod used up (SU-100) parts inventory that was previously produced... The uncertainty regarding SAU production in the near future has influenced the general course of production. The workforce at the plant literally "melts

The antenna housing with a hinged bottom section (for water drainage) and the damping device for the 9RS radio station antenna.

The fuel filler caps for the front fuel tanks. The diameter of the fuel filler cap was increased from October 1945. The early type (left) is 90mm diameter, the later type (right) is 120mm diameter.

The later type SU-100 commander's cupola with a single piece hatch, introduced in November 1945. The diameter of the new commander's cupola was increased, so eliminating the distinctive 20mm ledge located immediately under the old type cupola. The rectangular "patch" welded to the sponson is a characteristic feature of SU-100s produced at Plant №174 in Omsk.

The early type SU-100 commander's cupola with a double-leaf hatch. (A. Buylov)

Torsion bar assistance for the loader's hatch was tested in October and introduced on series production SU-100s from December 1945.

Tow hooks and latches, from left to right: an early design from the SU-85 used until the end of 1944; simplified latch design used until May 1945. The tow hooks were modified from May 1945, and from October 1945 a wire handle was added to the latch to facilitate easier opening of the latch.

away". At the same time, their work is curtailed by (lack of input from) the technical departments, the design office and production department. The majority of the KB (design department) has left the plant in the last months. Particularly bad is the situation with the technical (quality/acceptance) control due to the dismissal of a large number of supervisors, foremen and even the workshop chiefs from the plant".

In the circumstances described, it is unsurprising that all work on improving the SU-100 was quietly terminated at UZTM in anticipation of further immediate post-war changes to civil production, where available, and a reduced volume of military production at the plant generally. As production of SU-100 was being terminated at UZTM in Sverdlovsk, it is therefore curious that production was actually transferred to Plant №174 rather than being stopped, and for reasons that have only recently been better understood.

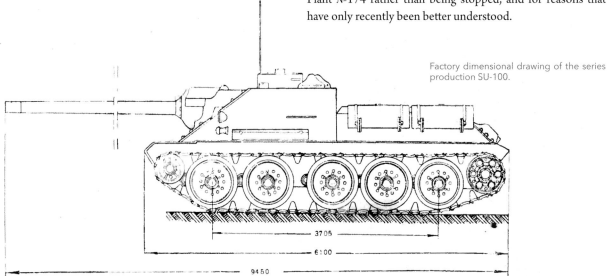

Factory dimensional drawing of the series production SU-100.

A late production SU-100 has its engine installed at the Uralmash plant production line. Note that the handrails have been moved to the middle of the engine compartment armoured side covers, characteristic of late production SU-100s in the absence of a handrail on the right side of the fighting compartment behind the sponson. (A. Bobkov collection)

Final inspection of a late production SU-100 at the UZTM plant in Sverdlovsk. The welded bolt-hole boss for fitting the self-extrication cable set is visible on the left side of the fighting compartment. The vertical oval blanking cover for connecting the track adjustment device of the front idler wheel is clearly visible on the right track guard. (S. Ageev collection)

Chapter 4

SU-100 Self-Propelled Gun Production at Omsk Plant №174

At the beginning of the Great Patriotic War, Plant №174 (the Voroshilov plant) was located in Leningrad, where it built the T-26 light tank and had also developed the replacement for the T-26, the altogether heavier T-50. In August 1941 the plant was evacuated to Siberia, with part of the production plant being re-established in Omsk, where in March 1942 it was combined with the local Plant №173 under a single plant number, Plant №174. Tank plant №173 had in turn been created on the basis of the Omsk Locomotive Plant in the name of Rudzutak (PVRZ), which had been amalgamated with the Voroshilovgrad locomotive plant named after the October Revolution (VZOR) evacuated from Leningrad. That plant had originally been located in Voroshilovgrad (from 1935-58 known as Lugansk, as it is again today). The movement of Soviet military production plants in the dar-

kest months of the Second World War is in of itself a military achievement almost beyond comprehension in its operational complexity.

The result of the above relocation and re-establishment of steel production and finishing facilities together with evacuated tank production plants was that a new integrated tank production facility was created in Omsk in June 1942 from three separate plants that also began to assemble T-34 tanks for the Red Army. Plant №174 latterly produced the T-34-85 tank from 1944-46 and also built T-34 generic components. But in an immediate post-war economic situation no different to that being experienced by UZTM at Sverdlovsk, and at a time that plant had ceased production of its own indigenous SU-100 design, Plant №174 surprisingly became a new start-up producer of the already terminated UZTM SU-100. It has only

SU-100s of Plant №174 production on parade in Red Square, Moscow 1ˢᵗ May 1951. Omsk production SU-100s were distinguished by characteristic front tow hook shape and the rectangular "patch" welded to the sponson. The storage container for crew personal kit has been removed for parade purposes. Note the mirror near the driver-mechanic's hatch to assist with column alignment during parades.

SU-100s of Plant №174 production on parade in Red Square, Moscow, 1st May 1951. These SU-100s are fitted with 6.5m tow cables.

SU-100s of Plant №174 production on parade in Red Square, Moscow, 1st May 1951. None of these SU-100s are fitted with crew personal kit containers.

recently been established that the SU-100 was in fact produced post-war at Omsk, and why such an apparently illogical move to re-establish assembly of an already terminated vehicle was undertaken. As always, there was inarguable logic behind the apparently incomprehensible decision.

In 1947, the Omsk tank plant began series production of the inherited UZTM SU-100 design, with production continuing until early 1948, during which period a relatively small (in Soviet terms) batch of 204 SU-100s was built, comparable to the wartime monthly output of the Uralmash plant at Sverdlovsk. The apparent lack of logic in transferring production from Sverdlovsk to Omsk led some modern historians for many years to conclude that the Omsk plant never actually built the SU-100. However, as was often the case in the Soviet Union, the unlikely was in fact the reality. SU-100 production

should logically have ended with the last units being assembled at Sverdlovsk. During the war, the appearance of the T-34 armed with its 85mm armament had put an end to the short career of the SU-85 armed with a gun of identical calibre. Similarly, after development of the T-54 armed with a 100mm tank gun, the SU-100 had also lost its relevance; as given equal firepower, a turreted tank is always the preferable installation option for any given calibre. Recent research has shown that the SU-100 was nevertheless produced at Omsk post-war, in parallel with the T-54 entering service with the Soviet Army. The Russian economics ministry (RGAE) archives contain records on the Plant №174 produced SU-100, while there are surviving SU-100s which have Omsk plant characteristic design features and Omsk serial numbers (in particular examples at the Central Armed Forces Museum in Moscow, the Lenino-Snegiri Museum near Dedovsk in the western suburbs of Moscow and the surviving SU-100 at Kubinka). The reasoning for this final "spurious" SU-100 production run at Plant №174 which seems strange today was actually a reasonable and logical decision in 1947.

Upon completion of the T-34-85 production program, Plant №174 was in 1947 expected to re-tool for production of a new tank type - the T-54. In that first year of T-54 series production, the three tank plants to be involved in T-54 assembly, namely Plant №183 (Nizhny Tagil), Plant №75 (Kharkov) and Plant №174 in Omsk were expected to assemble a total of 400 series production T-54 tanks, but in fact only 22 were completed, and all of those at the main plant, Plant №183 in Nizhny Tagil.

The first drawings of the new "Tagil" tank arrived at the Omsk plant only in September, and a complete approved set of drawings, production documents and technological condi-

tions were received only at the end of November 1947. After the end of the war, the situation at the Omsk plant was even worse than that at UZTM in Sverdlovsk. In May 1945, the party officials at the plant reported to the Central Committee of the CPSU (b) (the Communist (Bolshevik) Party of the Soviet Union) that plant workers based in Omsk were, as at UZTM in Sverdlovsk, voluntarily leaving the plant "based on the end of the war". There was a lack of assembly work, and thereby employment and workers had a strong desire to return home. Of the 12,385 designers, engineers and production staff working at Plant №174, as many as 96% had originally been evacuated from Leningrad, Voroshilovgrad, Stalingrad and other cities, and they quite naturally wanted to go home. Moreover, in Omsk the living conditions the workers had endured were far from ideal - shared dormitories and huts with bunk beds and limited family quarters. With the post-war decrease in the

SU-100s of Plant №174 production on parade in Red Square, Moscow, 7th November 1951 parade. These SU-100s are fitted with crew personal kit containers.

An SU-100 of typical Plant №174 production configuration. Note the BDSh-5 smoke containers mounted on the rear armour plate.

The SU-100 as produced at Plant №174 plant featured distinctively wide rear armour plate hinges. The armoured exhaust covers as produced at Plant №174 in Omsk were also shorter than those mounted on UZTM produced SU-100s. The distance from the lower edge of the exhaust covers to the edge of the armour plate was increased to 400mm (the exhaust cover mounting holes in the rear armour plate were unchanged between UZTM and Plant №174 production, only the cover length was different).

The rear armour plate hinges and armoured exhaust covers of the UZTM production SU-100 for comparison. The distance from the lower edge of the exhaust covers to the edge of the armour plate was 350mm on UZTM produced SU-100s.

The driver-mechanic's hatch of an SU-100 produced at Plant №174. Note the part number cast on the hinge mounting, specific to Plant №174 production. The driver-mechanic's hatch hinge mounting on UZTM produced SU-100s lacked this feature.

The shorter armoured exhaust covers as mounted on SU-100s produced at Plant №174.

The armoured cupola over the gun recoil system on the roof of Plant №174 produced SU-100's also had cast part numbers. Early Omsk production SU-100s were marked 71 Л 100 29 098 3. This SU-100 is from May 1947 production.

Later Omsk production SU-100s were marked Л 71 100 29 0 98 3. This SU-100 is from July 1947 production. (A. Buylov)

The armoured cupola over the gun recoil system on UZTM production SU-100's were by comparison unmarked.

volume of military production, salaries had also fallen sharply, and simply having sufficient money to buy food in the marketplaces in Siberia (where nearly all food was imported from other regions) in order to live reasonably had become an issue. This had been accepted by plant workers during the war as an inevitability of the circumstances. But post-war, such hardships were not taken as obligatory and people began to leave the military production cities in Siberia in large numbers. It was within this economic situation that the decision was taken to undertake temporary production of the SU-100 at Plant №174 in Omsk. The main reason as alluded to earlier was to retain skilled tank production workers - in fact skilled workers in general - in Siberia where the production plants had been relocated during the war.

With regard to Plant №174 re-tooling for post-war SU-100 assembly, the SU-100 chassis was from a production perspective basically the same as the T-34-85 recently produced at Omsk, and the 100mm D-10S (SK) gun was almost identical to the 100mm D-10T tank gun version then being developed

for installation in the T-54 being prepared for series production at the same plant. The SU-100 drawings were transferred from the Uralmash factory, but Plant №174 adapted SU-100 production to the manufacturing techniques and locally procured components employed during its own prior T-34-85 production experience. The Omsk produced SU-100, designated "Obiekt-138" had some specific design features that differed from the Sverdlovsk produced SU-100. The hull floor was constructed of three armour plates (instead of five on the UZTM produced SU-100). It had tow hooks of a characteristic shape, the box section front mudguards of post-war UZTM production, short armoured exhaust pipe covers, unified transmission access and rear armour plate hinges and other detail differences from the UZTM built SU-100. The design changes undertaken within the short period of SU-100 production Omsk were not specifically detailed and documentet in the way they were at UZTM.

The early armoured final drive housing (left) compared with the later type (right). The protruding bolt is removed to check the oil level.

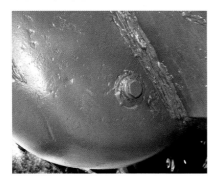

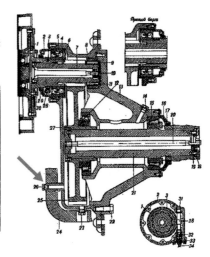

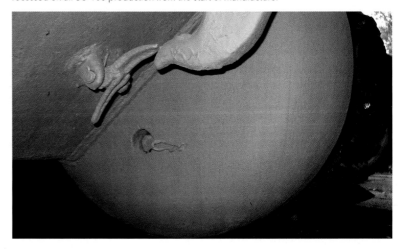

The later armoured final drive housing as produced from the summer of 1947. The oil-level monitoring plug bolt head has been recessed to prevent damage. The oil drain plug was recessed on all SU-100 production from the start of manufacture.

From left to right: 1. UZTM production tracks - the most common type used during wartime, and in the immediate post-war era. 2. Post-war SU-100 Plant №174 production track - with added transverse stiffening. 3 and 4. A typical post-war repair with track links of different types.

The road wheel arm travel limiters on SU-100s produced at Plant №174 were welded vertically.

The road wheel arm travel limiters on SU-100s produced at UZTM were welded at an angle.

The front tow hook used on SU-100s of Plant №174 (Omsk) production.

By comparison, the front tow hook used on SU-100s of UZTM plant production, with a distinctive protruding ridge.

Chapter 5

Post-War SU-100 Modernisation

The SU-100 was modernised in the Soviet Union in parallel with, and to the same standards as, the T-34-85. These upgrades were in several stages, beginning in the late 1940s and continuing into the 1960s, and even later.

Post-War 1940s Modernisation

In the immediate post-war era, it was expected that wartime T-34 tanks and self-propelled guns based on the T-34 chassis would be quickly replaced by more modern alternatives. In practice however, some World War Two vintage armoured vehicles remained in service almost until the middle of 1980s, albeit with significant modernisations and modifications.

Modernisation was generally carried out in parallel with capital repair at the plants of the Main Armoured Directorate (GBTU), with the modernisations to be undertaken centrally dictated, as for all types of armoured vehicles in service with the Soviet Army at the time. Such project work was for example undertaken until 1962 at the Moscow Central Experimental Plant №1 GBTU and Research Institute VNII-100, and for the SU-100 at Plant №174 in Omsk (renamed the October Revolution Plant from 1965). Modernisations common to both the T-34-85 and SU-100 were approved by the KB at Plant №183 in Nizhny Tagil under the leadership of chief designer L. N. Kartsev.

It is not possible to accurately track the exact implementation date of all post-war improvements on the SU-100, as they were carried out on different vehicles at different times as they arrived in maintenance workshops for capital repair or rebuild. The updated SU-100s (Obiekt-138) did not receive any specific nomenclature or index, and the modernisation stages were also unnamed. They are separated here by year(s) of introduction, but this is to a certain extent arbitrary, as not all SU-100s

A column of Soviet Army SU-100 self-propelled guns on the move in 1956. The vehicles have the later angular track guards and other post-war details such as the FG-102 headlamp, but no crew personal effects containers.

were modernised. Some general patterns can nevertheless be identified. One of the most obvious post-war changes to the appearance of the SU-100 was the introduction of an angular container for crew personal belongings, which was mounted on the right track guard of all SU-100s ahead of the commander's sponson.

There were also some relatively obscure modifications. From the summer of 1947, the oil level-check blanking plug on the cast final drive housings was changed from a protruding bolt to a flush blanking plug on the SU-100s produced at Plant №174 in Omsk. The need to repair these massive assemblies was obviously rare, but at least one SU-100 originally produced by UZTM had a final drive housing replaced with an Omsk type.

From March 1945, Plant №183 in Nizhny Tagil began to produce T-34-85 drive wheels with a slightly larger diameter

of 650mm, replacing the earlier 634mm type. The diameter of axis of the rollers that engaged with the track link guide horns remained unchanged at 492mm as on the earlier type drive wheel. The wheel outer diameter was increased to improve the rotation of the track links around the drive wheel, and to reduce wear on the track teeth. The reason for this subtle engineering change was that the track pitch was 172mm on new track, but the track quickly wore down and deformed in service, so increasing the pitch, as a consequence of which the drive wheel rollers began to "catch" the track link guide horns closer to the base of the guide horn, and with sharper blows. This also gave the T-34 its distinctive "track clank" on the move. Plant №174 in Omsk apparently did not produce the later 650mm diameter wheels, but during repairs SU-100s were sometimes fitted with new "T-34" drive wheels from Plant №183.

Central wheel hub cap blanking bolts and washers were added to the main road wheels by Plant №183 in Nizhny Tagil from 3rd October 1945, so as to provide easier bearing lubrication. The final production SU-100s built by the Plant №174 were apparently also fitted with these hub cap blanking bolts ex-works, but en-masse they appeared on all SU-100s only in 1950-51 during capital repairs.

1950s Modernisation

During the 1950s, some SU-100s were modernised at Tankovo Remontniye Zavodi (TRZ) - capital repair plants. Worn road wheels were sometimes replaced with cast wheels from the T-44A, with the "spider" type of finned road wheel produced by Plant №183. From the beginning of the 1950s (not later than 1952 as indicated on the original drawings) a rear facing GST-49 convoy lamp with white light filter was fitted on

The hinged track guard used on Omsk production SU-100s, with an eight-section hinge.

The standardised hinged track guard used at tank repair plants during capital repair of all T-34 tanks and SPGs on the T-34 chassis. Note the ten-section hinge.

The fixed section of the hinged track guard part was attached to the glacis plate. To incline the movable track guard, it was sufficient to unscrew a single bolt.

the roof of the fighting compartment facing rearward. From 1952, the 9RS radio set and TPU-3-Bis-f tank intercom were replaced respectively by the 10RT-26Eh radio set and TPU-47 intercom.

In 1955 a water-tube boiler type engine pre-heater, directly linked to the engine cooling system, was fitted in the fighting compartment directly behind the commander's seat. A special hatch equipped with a hinged lid and protected from impact by a welded guard was cut in the hull floor next to the emergency hatch for the exhaust from this pre-heater. The "heated coolant" was circulated by a pump through not only the cylinder blocks, but also through special radiators installed in the oil lubricant tanks. The latter installation reduced the capacity of each of the two oil lubrication tanks from 40 to 38 litres, and the entire lubrication system from 105 to 100 litres. The V-2 diesel engine's oil consumption was as previously mentioned

significant – per Soviet records it was 20 ml/hp/hour - which in layman's terms meant that when operating at 400hp the engine consumed a not insignificant 8 litres of MT-16P oil for every operating hour. Any reduction in the lubrication system capacity was thereby undesirable. As a remedial measure, one of the two external 90-litre fuel tanks on the left side (usually the rear one) was used for transporting spare lubrication oil, and marked accordingly.

During capital repair, worn original V-2-34 engines were often replaced by the modernised V-2-34M or V-2-34M11, fitted with a NK-10 fuel transfer pump and (from 1955) the VTI-3 two stage multi-cyclone dust collection and ejection system. The original VG-4 type signal horn, located next to the headlight was from 1956 replaced by the S-56 type (this signal horn was also used on military vehicles such as the GAZ-51/63, GAZ-69, ZiS-150 and ZiL-157).

As part of the capital rebuild program begun at the beginning of the 1950s, a rear facing GST-64 marker light with white glass filter was mounted on the SU-100 fighting compartment roof.

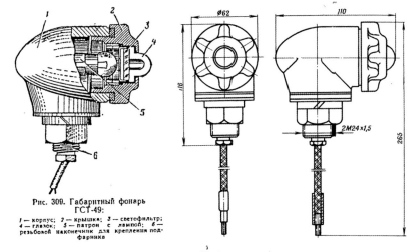

Рис. 309. Габаритный фонарь ГСТ-49:

1 — корпус; 2 — крышка; 3 — светофильтр; 4 — глазок; 5 — патрон с лампой; 6 — резьбовой наконечник для крепления подфарника

715. Светильник ГСТ-64-3 54.26.436 и ГСТ-64-К 54.26.54

The "GST-49" and later "GST-64" marker lights are very similar, hence the designers took the trouble to mould the characters into the casing.

Features of the modern SU-100 upgraded for parade purposes, with a set of GST-64 marker lights with white glass filters at the rear. (A. Aksenov)

The FG-10 headlamp (left), the FG-100 "100 series" with sealed optical element (centre), and the infra-red FG-102 (right).

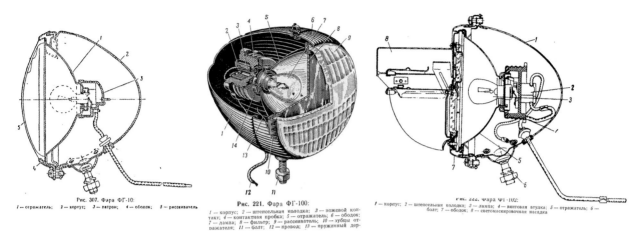

Рис. 307. Фара ФГ-10:

1 — отражатель; 2 — корпус; 3 — патрон; 4 — ободок; 5 — рассеиватель

Рис. 221. Фара ФГ-100:

1 — корпус; 2 — штепсельная колодка; 3 — ножевой контакт; 4 — контактная пробка; 5 — отражатель; 6 — ободок; 7 — лампа; 8 — фильтр; 9 — рассеиватель; 10 — зубцы отражателя; 11 — болт; 12 — провод; 13 — пружинный дер-

Рис. 222. Фара ФГ-102:

1 — корпус; 2 — штепсельная колодка; 3 — лампа; 4 — винтовая втулка; 5 — отражатель; 6 — болт; 7 — ободок; 8 — светомаскировочная насадка

The FG-125 headlamp (left) and the infra-red FG-127 (right).

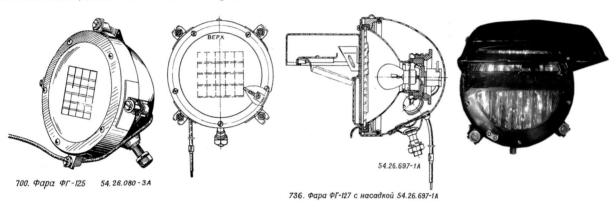

700. Фара ФГ-125   54.26.080-3А

54.26.697-1А

736. Фара ФГ-127 с насадкой 54.26.697-1А

An SU-100 with features added for modern military parade purposes. An additional escort light is mounted on the fighting compartment rear near the external telephone socket, replacing the original GST light. Interestingly, this is an upgraded early SU-100 - produced no later than January 1945, still in service for parade purposes in the 21st Century. (A. Aksenov)

A modern FG-127 headlamp on an SU-100 rebuilt for modern era parades. (A. Aksenov)

A pair of GST-64 convoy lights are also mounted on the glacis armour plate on modern "parade" rebuilds. Note the large rectangular mirror near the driver-mechanic's hatch for maintaining column alignment. The mounting brackets for the lower pair of shovels (from the 1960s upgrade) have been removed. All SU-100s modified for parade purposes have had their pioneer tools and tow cables removed. The left headlight is a modern FG-127 and a modern S-314 horn is fitted. All wheels are from the T-44M, and the ASh-4 radio antenna has been moved to the fighting compartment roof. (A. Aksenov)

1960s Modernisation

In 1958, trials were conducted with the T-54 MBT to determine the feasibility of increasing the range and autonomy of tank regiments from "tyl" rear supply forces by means of providing additional external rear hull mounted fuel tanks. Brackets were added for mounting two standard 200-litre fuel drums, and this solution was universally adopted on other tanks. On the T-34 and SU-100, the revision was included on tanks undergoing capital repair from 1960. The brackets for the barrels were mounted where the BDSh-5 smoke canisters had been mounted previously. The BDSh-5 smoke canisters were during long marches now attached to newly welded mounting points located on the engine deck side covers, near the rear wall of the fighting compartment.

The external fuel canisters mounted on the rear of the SU-100 were post-war still not directly plumbed into the fuel system of the SU-100, remaining simply storage drums rather than system fuel tanks. The crew now needed to consider the transfer of another 400 litres of fuel from external canisters into the main fuel system, which was obviously less laborious if the manual pump was replaced with an electric type.

As part of the 1960s modernisation program, an MZA-3 compact transfer pump was added to the SU-100, which was placed in a special metal container when not in use. The attachment mountings for this box were usually welded on the right side of the fighting compartment behind the commander's cupola sponson (for which mounting the handrail was removed on some SU-100s), but occasionally this box was mounted on the left side at tank repair plants as with T-34-85s modernised at that time. A hull mounted external electrical socket was provided for connecting the MZA-3 pump, a portable lamp or for starting the engine from an external battery. Within the fra-

Overhead view of the BVN night vision device tube.

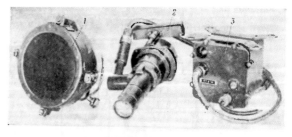

Рис. 55. Комплект прибора БВН:
1 — фара ФГ-125; 2 — прибор наблюдения БВН; 3 — блок питания БТ-6-26

The driver-mechanic's BVN night vision set was installed on the SU-100 from 1959. Here, the late type BVN with FG-125 headlamp as an infrared illuminator.

An infra-red night vision lamp mounted on the right side of the SU-100. The lamp was normally mounted on the left side.

The mounting bracket for the electrical wires for the additional starboard headlamp as added during the 1960 upgrade program.

mework of this modernisation, the self-extraction equipment located on the left side of the fighting compartment since 1945 was removed and replaced with four large shovels (one for each of the crew) and a pick-shovel, which became the standard set of entrenching tools on Soviet tanks of the time. Initially the T-34 and SU-100 had only a single shovel on the right track guard. The two-handed saw was left in place.

In the 1960s, worn road wheels (usually the first two wheel stations were badly affected) began to be changed with wheels from the T-44M tank. The latter wheels had the same general appearance as the T-54 and the later T-55 and T-62 - referred to abroad but not in the Soviet Union as "starfish" - but these wheels were not identical to the T-54/55 type, being

of larger diameter and with a thinner profile. The solid rubber tyre rimmed T-34/T-44 wheel had a diameter of 830mm and profile of 150mm versus 810mm and 185mm respectively for the T-54/T-55. The wheels also used different bearings and had a different number of bolts on the hub (the T-34/T-44 had five, the T-54 had six).

From 1959, the SU-100 driver-mechanic was provided with a BVN night vision device, illuminated by an FG-100 headlight with an infra-red filter. The FG-100 began to be mounted set on the right side of the front armoured plate (the presence of a bracket for it and cable output is one of the signs of an SU-100 having undergone modernisation in the 1960s). The BVN night vision device, when in working position, was

1. The early type electric VG-4 signal horn.

2. The S-56-G electric signal horn installed on SU-100s rebuilt from 1956.

3. The S-58 electric waterproof signal horn installed on SU-100s rebuilt from 1960.

4. The modern S-313 electric waterproof signal horn used on SU-100s restored specifically to participate in military parades.

fastened in the opening of the driver-mechanic's hatch on a special removable bracket. The hatch could not be closed with the BVN device in use.

The left headlight was also changed to the "100" series FG-102 headlight with a blackout mask (in Russian - SMU). Externally the new headlights were almost identical to the previous series FG-10 headlight (when with SMU - FG-26), but with a sealed beam optical element. Interestingly, sometimes on older photographs the right headlight can be seen with an SMU blackout mask and the left headlight with an infrared filter. The S-56 signal horn was in 1960 replaced by the S-58 type, in a moisture-proof enclosure, as used on other military vehicles such as the MAZ-535 wheeled tractor.

As part of the same 1960s modernisation program, the commander's Mk.4 periscope viewing device was replaced with a TPK-1 binocular viewing device. This had been fitted to modern tanks since 1949, but was from the 1960s retroactively applied to older armoured vehicles. The periscope binoculars provided 5x magnification, more than doubling target recognition range from 1-1.5km to 3km.

Already in 1954, Soviet tanks were being fitted with a new set of communications equipment, the R-113 "Granat" radio set, R-120 intercom and ASh-4 antenna. The T-34-85 and SU-100 were then serving in first line units, but were already considered obsolete, so were not upgraded until much later. The T-34-85 was equipped with the R-113 radio set from 1957, but as late as at the end 1960s the SU-100 still often used the old 10PT-26E radio set. An example recorded for posterity is that of line service SU-100s of the 8th Tank Army of the Carpathian Military District, which were used in the Soviet 1968 film "Na voine kak na voine" (At war like at war). The Plant №174 (by now Omsk "October Revolution Plant") drawings show the R-113 installation upgrade recorded as being undertaken as late as 1967.

The new R-113 radio and R-120 intercom communi-

The hemispherical wheel hub cap design as used in SU-100 production at Plant №174. The central bolt was removed for bearing lubrication.

Two different wheel hub caps as used on all T-34 tanks and T-34 SAUs during post-war capital repairs.

The T-44M stamped "starfish" wheel, similar (but not identical) to that used on the T-54 and T-55 was also developed for retrofit to T-34-85 tanks and SU-100 SAUs during capital repairs.

The T-44A cast "spider" wheels as designed by Plant №183 for use during capital repair of the T-34-85 tank and SU-100 SAU. (A. Aksenov)

The engine pre-heater exhaust pipe hatch on the hull floor of the upgraded SU-100 from 1955 (position 14 on the drawing).

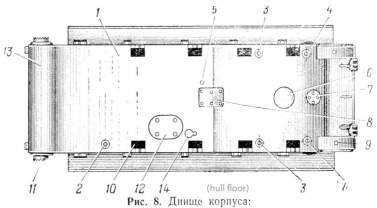

The engine pre-heater exhaust pipe hatch. The baffle is welded ahead of the hatch to protect from damage by uneven ground and other obstacles.

Рис. 8. Днище корпуса:

1 — днище; *2* — пробка лючка для слива топлива из переднего бака; *3* — пробка лючка для слива масла; *4* — пробка лючка для слива топлива из бортовых баков; *5* — отверстие для слива воды; *6* — колпак под вентилятором; *7* — крышка лючка для слива масла из коробки передач; *8* — крышка лючка под двигателем; *9* — пробка для слива масла из бортовых передач; *10* — вырез шахты; *11* — кронштейны направляющего колеса; *12* — крышка люка запасного выхода; *13* — нижний носовой лист; *14* — крышка лючка для выпуска продуктов сгорания из подогревателя

The engine pre-heater installation and its connection to the engine cooling system.

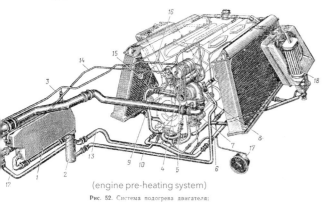

(engine pre-heating system)

Рис. 52. Система подогрева двигателя:

подогревателя; *2* — труба выпуска отработавших газов; *3* — паропроводная трубка; *4* — насосный узел; *5* — электро-; *6* — обогреваемый масляный трубопровод; *7* — маслозаливающий насос узла; *13* — трубопровод под-ная труба; *10* — трубопровод к котлу подогревателя; *11* — форсунка; *12* — свеча накаливания; *13* — трубопровод под-чей жидкости из котла в систему; *14* — топливная трубка для подачи топлива к насосу подогревателя; *17* — указатель температуры; *18* — теплообменник

These two external 90 litre fuel tanks are representative of the wartime type (left) and the post-war type with the filler offset to one end of the tank (right),

cations set was configured for four crew rather than three as previously. The loader as before did not have a headset. An external socket was located on the fighting compartment roof by which the commander of a "desant" infantry contingent riding on the SU-100 could communicate with the crew. This socket mounting varied somewhat, but was usually installed near the convoy (clearance) lamp (the GST-49 had by this time been replaced by a GST-64 lamp with red filter) or on the left side of the fighting compartment roof. At some point in the 1960s, new external 90-litre fuel tanks were fitted, with the fuel filler moved from the middle to the end of each tank.

From 1967, the FG-100 and FG-102 headlamps were re-placed respectively by the FG-125 and FG-127 with the SMU blackout mask. After 1969, some SU-100s were provided with the more sophisticated TVN-2 "Ugol" (corner) night vision device for the driver-mechanic (introduction into service in 1957 and also mounted on the T-54 MBT and T-10 heavy tank). Judging by the remaining fixtures on the commander's cupolas (probably for an OU-3 infra-red illuminator) that remain on the preserved Plant №174 production SU-100 at the Lenino-Sne-giri Museum and another late Omsk production SU-100 located at Kubinka, it can be assumed that some SU-100s were latterly equipped with the TKN-1 (or TKN-2) commander's night vision devices.

1970s and 1980s Modernisation

By the 1970s, the SU-100 had long-since been relegated from operational service in the Soviet Army, but some SU-100s remained in service in training units, and in military long-term strategic storage. There is no accurate data on the modernisation undertaken at this late time, as such work was performed locally on single or small batches of self-propelled guns. These later conversions were in some cases for special purposes, such as conversion to self-propelled targets, and later for participation in late Soviet era, and post-Soviet Russian, Victory Day parades.

An inverted U-shaped frame was welded on the rear wall of the fighting compartment of all SU-100s during the 1970s. This was for mounting the 52-021 universal double-action pump in the operating position. The pump was used for both liquid and air charging of the gun recuperation mechanism. The same inverted U-shaped frame was introduced on all self-propelled guns and towed guns (such as the M-30, etc.) in order to standardise maintenance, as different artillery systems had previously been equipped with different pumps types. Some SU-100s were at the time also upgraded with the R-123 radio station and R-124 intercommunication system.

1985 Victory Parade

For the 40th anniversary Victory Day parade on Moscow's Red Square planned for 9th May 1985, the decision was taken to begin the mechanised part of the parade with a historical section featuring armoured vehicles and equipment from the era of the Great Patriotic War. A quantity of T-34-85s and SU-100s were chosen to participate in the parade, which were removed from long-term strategic storage and refurbished. Among the SU-100s chosen for the parade were machines from different production periods that differed significantly in detail. They all however featured traces of earlier post-war upgrades.

For the purposes of representing "historic vehicles" at a modern military parade the post-war GTS-64 clearance lamps were removed, and replaced with FG-125 so-called "convoy

The MDSh smoke canisters were relocated on the roof of the engine compartment during the 1960 capital upgrade program because post 1960 the 200 litre fuel tanks were now mounted in their previous position.

The storage box for the MZA-3 compact electric fuel pump as provided as part of the 1960s upgrade program - in a typical mounting position for the SU-100. (A. Aksenov)

The storage box for the MZA-3 compact electric fuel pump was sometimes located on the left side of the fighting compartment. During the 1960s upgrade program this box was also sometimes placed in the same location as on concurrent T-34-85s.

lights". In service, a red filter was placed in front of the lens glass with a stencil with the tactical number, clearly visible even at night. The SU-100s used for the parade featured the standard transparent glass.

To comply with current road regulations, the SU-100s were fitted with two GTS-64 marker lights on the front armour plate and another two on the rear. Curiously, all were fitted with white light filters, although modern rules require green lenses for blackout on the forward lights and red for the rear pair. The radio antenna input (for the R-113 or R-123 radio set) on these machines was moved to the roof of the commander's sponson and cupola, and the output under the old antenna input on the right side of the hull was patch welded. SU-100s modified in this manner have since 1985 periodically participated in the 9th May Victory Day parades on Red Square, most recently in on 24th June 2020.

The electrical requirements for external battery engine-starting, use of the MZA-3 pump etc. required a conduit, for which an extra hole was made in the hinged frame of the rear radiator grille cover (to the left of the red tail-light).

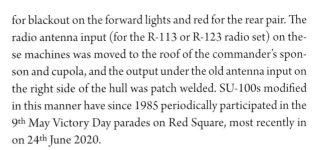

The electrical outlet and tail-light bracket.

This SU-100 was for unknown reasons not equipped with an electric socket during the 1960s upgrade program. Only a cutout for the tail-light is evident.

A typical 1960s upgrade, with a common large cutout for both the electrical outlet and the tail-light.

The composition and location of "pioneer" tooling was changed during the 1960s upgrade program. The location previously used to locate the self-extrication equipment on the left side of the fighting compartment was now used to mount four large shovels and a pick-axe.

This typical "museum exhibit" SU-100, in this instance an SAU produced in June 1945, bears the traces of upgrading over the years. 1. Traces of the original welded mountings for self-extrication equipment. 2. Traces of welded mountings for four shovels and a pick-axe.

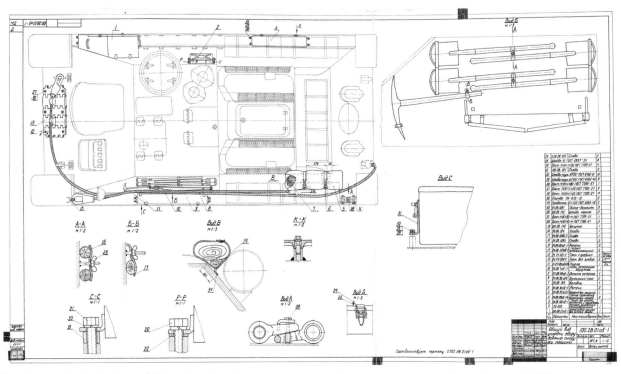

Plant drawing showing the layout of "pioneer" tooling and parts in accordance with the upgrade program carried out in the early 1960s.

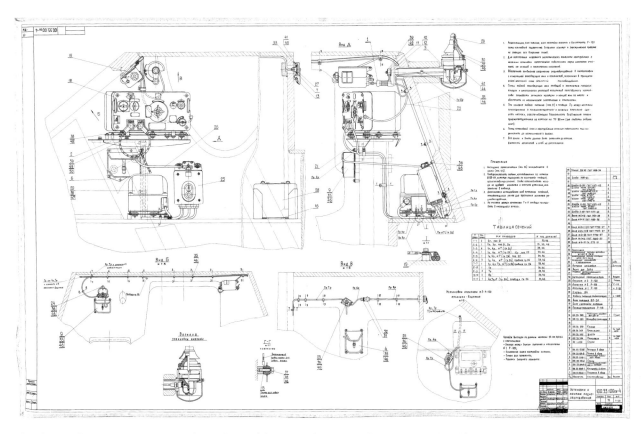

Plant drawing illustrating the requirements for installation of the R-113 radio station in the SU-100, introduced from 1967.

The R-113 radio installation included a new R-120 four-unit tank TPU intercom system including the ability to communicate with the SU-100 crew from outside the vehicle. The telephone socket linked to the commander's telephone was placed on the fighting compartment roof next to the GTS marker light, or on the rear wall. Sometimes a guard was fitted, sometimes not.

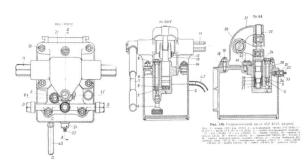

A service manual drawing showing the 52-I-021 double action pump for replenishing the gun recoil system.

The mounting bracket for the 52-I-021 double-acting pump was welded to the fighting compartment rear wall of all SU-100s from the 1970s. The location varied, depending in part on whether the vertical section of the loader's hatch was present or not. (A. Buylov)

The same mounting bracket for a double-acting recharge pump was used on towed artillery such as this 122mm M-30 howitzer.

Chapter 6

Operational Service

The first production SU-100s were not immediately issued to combat units. The SU-100 entered service with the Red Army in September 1944, but the first production units were delivered for training purposes to military schools while the 100mm armour-piercing ammunition supply problem was being remedied. SU-100s began to be formed into SAU (self-propelled artillery) combat regiments from November. The first three SAU brigades - Russian abbreviation SABr - were formed in December 1944, with 65 SU-100s in each brigade.

In November 1944, self-propelled artillery regiments - Russian abbreviation SAP (P-polk) - of the Reserv Verkhnogo Glavnogo Kommandovaniya - the Supreme High Command Reserve (RVGK) which had been previously armed with the SU-85 began to be reorganised in accordance with manning table №010/462, which designated that each SAU regiment was to have a total of 20 SU-85 or SU-100 SAUs organised into four batteries, each equipped with five SU-85 or SU-100 SAUs, plus one regimental commander's vehicle (in the earlier manning table №010/483 dating from 1943, the commander's vehicle was a T-34 tank rather than a SAU). Due to the large number of separate self-propelled artillery regiments that were in service, there were some operational difficulties with focusing self-propelled artillery where required in key areas and in organising the associated logistics. A decision was therefore taken in January 1944 to create brigade level self-propelled artillery units for command and control purposes, which consisted of up to three self-propelled artillery regiments under their overall command.

Three medium self-propelled artillery RVGK brigades with three regiments in each were formed in winter of 1944-45. 65 SU-100s and three SU-76s (for commanders) were located in each of these brigades, and they were formed on the basis of the already existing 1st Leningradskaya Tank Brigade (renamed the 207th Leningradskaya Self-Propelled Artillery

This SU-100 with the tactical number 433 was built in the winter of 1944-1945. It was photographed in Prague in May 1945.

Brigade of the RVGK, formed in Orienbaum, on 18th December), the 118th Dvinskaya Tank Brigade (renamed the 208th Dvinskaya Self-Propelled Artillery Brigade RVGK - formed on 24th January 1945) and 122nd Tank Brigade (renamed the 209th Self-Propelled Artillery Brigade of the RVGK, formed on 9th December 1944). All three brigades were sent to front in early February 1945, with the 207th and 209th becoming part of the 2nd Ukrainian Front, while the 208th became integral to the 3rd Ukrainian Front.

In the spring of 1945 a fourth self-propelled artillery brigade, the 231st brigade, was formed in the Belorussian-Lithuanian Military District (BLVO), armed with the SU-100. The 231st brigade did not take part in the war against Germany, but was within the 6th Guards Tank Army of the Transbaikal Front involved in later fighting against the Japanese. Self-Propelled Artillery Brigade №231 was awarded the honorary title "Khingansky" on 20th September 1945 for successful combat operations in the Far East during the break-through in the Manjaro-Kalinovski and Halon-Orshanski fortified sector, in crossing the Great Khingan mountain range and for the relief of the cities of Changchun, Mukden, Qiqihar, Rehe, Dairen and Port Arthur.

In addition to these four brigades (SABr), another 120 medium self-propelled artillery regiments (SAP) were formed before the end of the war, some of which became integral to

separate anti-tank artillery brigades of the RVGK, others were used to strengthen tank and mechanised corps.

Combat Debut

The first major campaign in which SU-100s participated was the Budapest strategic offensive operation, in which 59 SU-100s were involved, from three regiments, namely the 382nd Guards SAP, formed in September under the command of Guards Major Efim Mikhailovich Mikheev, the 1453rd SAP under the command of Major Victor K. Petukhov and the 1821st SAP under the command of Colonel Dmitry Pavlovich Gromov. They were all in early January 1945 transferred to the 1st Guards Mechanised Corps under the command of Lieutenant-General Ivan Nikitich Russiyanov, which was part of the 3rd Ukrainian Front.

The first battle involving SU-100s of the 382nd SAP took place on 7th January* in the town of Zsámbék, 30km west of Budapest, during the German "Konrad I" offensive to relieve the blockade of Budapest. During this first battle, SU-100s were forced to repel a German attack without infantry support because a platoon of the 49th infantry division had been dispersed under enemy fire. The SU-100 crews fought virtually without other supporting units against 30 tanks and a battalion of Wehrmacht infantry. During this first battle one of the

A column of SU-85Ms in the final days of the Third Reich in Germany. The vulnerable "long march" fuel tanks were removed during street fighting. The SU-85M and SU-100M were from some angles difficult to distinguish. Note the "SU-100" chassis twin ventilator housing on the fighting compartment roof, and the stowed shell casings.

*Recent Russian sources indicate that units from the 1453rd Self-Propelled Artillery Brigade clashed with Panthers from the 5. SS. Pz. Division as early as 5th January in the area of Biscke, Hungary.

main drawbacks of the SU-100 became clear - namely the lack of machine-guns for defensive fire. Except for their personal weapons and grenades, the crews had nothing to oppose the German infantry, who quickly circumvented the SU-100s and cut off the regiment from reinforcements. Some of the SU-100 crews were forced into hand-to-hand combat on the ground in the resulting fighting, with some SU-100s destroyed by German infantry using Molotov cocktails and anti-tank grenades. The battle lasted all day, with the German offensive eventually being repulsed. Enemy tank losses from direct SU-100 fire included four PzKpfw.V Panthers destroyed and another four da-

maged. The Soviet 382nd regiment had however lost nine SU-100s destroyed in combat, with two SU-100s badly damaged, representing a loss of more than half their available SAUs.

Two weeks later, SU-100s of the 382nd SAP participated in the defence of Székesfehérvár, repelling the German offensive of 19-25 January during the final German "Konrad III" operation to relieve the Budapest blockade. The 145th SAP was in the reserve and the SU-100s entered combat on 25th January against German Pz.VI "Tiger" and Pz.VI "King Tiger" heavy tanks of the SS panzer divisions "Viking" and "Totenkompf". The German "Konrad III" operation ultimately failed in the

SU-85Ms built on the SU-100 chassis, accompanied by T-34-85s and the relatively rare ISU-122S as the Red Army closed on Berlin in the spring of 1945.

An SU-85M of the 1295th Self-Propelled Artillery Regiment of the 9th Mechanised Corps of the 3rd Guards Tank Army, Germany, April 1945, during the battle of Berlin. The SU-85M was from some angles very difficult to distinguish from the SU-100.

same manner as the earlier "Konrad I and II", but the 1st Guards mechanised corps lost 17 SU-100s in the battle.

Describing the experience in January 1945, the artillery commander of the 1st Guards mechanised corps, Guards Colonel Zakharov, noted in a report dated 15th February 1945 that, despite the larger and more powerful 100mm D-10S installation, the crew working conditions within the SU-100 had not deteriorated in comparison with the SU-85, while the new SAU had comparable maneuverability and better running gear reliability. Despite the weight of the rounds used having almost doubled (from 16kg to 32.6kg) the rate of fire in combat remained a respectable 4-5 rounds per minute as against 7-8 rounds for the 85mm D-5S-85 mounted on the SU-85, while first hit kill probability was significantly higher. The ammunition stowage rack and commander's cupola were noted as improvements compared with the SU-85. The armour protection was increased, but it was noted that: *the frontal armour of the SU-100 is invulnerable from light and medium artillery fire but the frontal armour is insufficient to protect from heavy enemy tanks and artillery of 88mm calibre*. * Among the shortcomings noted was the tight working space for the gun laying mechanism and the vulnerability of the optics to impact damage from pro-

jectiles. Further to the combat engagements described in January, the report expressed the desire to have the SU-100 armed with a machine gun for self-defence against enemy infantry. In the interim, it was recommended to give each crew member a 7.62mm sub-machine or light machine gun, in addition, to 8-10 7.62mm DP light machine guns to the sub-machine gunner companies of self-propelled artillery regiments. The SU-100 report concluded that the SU-100 was *"the most effective means of dealing with enemy heavy tanks."*

The 207th, 208th and 209th Self-Propelled Artillery Brigades previously held in reserve partook in the Balaton defensive operation in March 1945, repelling the German "Spring Awakening" counter-offensive. The 207th and 209th self-propelled artillery brigades were thereafter transferred to the 3rd Ukrainian Front.

The 1068th regiment of the 208th brigade suffered heavy losses during an advance conducted on 9th March along the Tsetse-Székesfehérvár highway. The regiment had no advance intelligence as to the enemy disposition in the area, and ran directly into heavy German armour opposition, as a consequence of which the regiment lost 14 of its 21 SU-100s in the ensuing firefight.

An SU-100 belonging to the Red Army 59th Independent Tank Recovery Battalion. Unknown location, 1945. (Lee Archer)

* *(TsAMO, Fund 243, Inventory 2928, Case 147)*

An SU-100 moving through the streets of Berlin, April 1945 according to the original caption. The SAU is painted with the identification markings used during the battle for Berlin, however the vehicle is transporting passengers including two officers in what appear to be British or Polish uniforms and the cyclist seems remarkably unperturbed, suggesting a post-victory SU-100 "on tour". (Lee Archer)

The arrival of the liberators. An SU-100 belonging to the 2nd Ukrainian Front (probably to the 1st Guards Mechanised Corps) passes through a village on the way towards Prague on the morning 9th May 1945. (Petr Dolezal)

On 10th March, again in a defensive operation to repel a German counterattack, SU-100s of the 1951st and 1953rd regiments of the 209th brigade destroyed nine German tanks and SPGs. The 2nd battery of the 1952nd regiment of the 209th brigade under the command of Captain Vasiliev destroyed three "King Tiger" tanks from the 501st heavy tank battalion of the 1st SS Panzer Corps, without incurring any Soviet losses.

Due to the high level of tank losses in combat as the Red Army pushed ever closer to Berlin's Axis strongholds, the SU-100 was occasionally used for the direct support of infantry in combat. In such situations, the inappropriate use of SU-100s, which had limited traverse and no secondary defensive armament, resulted in heavy losses. When used as intended for long-range fire support and conventional ambushes, the SU-100 by comparison suffered relatively small losses.

In optimal circumstances, SU-100 SAU batteries were camouflaged among trees at the edges of woods or on the reverse slopes of low heights, moving to their combat positions located within 100-200m of cover only on command from an observation post after the appearance of enemy forces. After firing a few rounds, the SU-100s would return to shelter without waiting for the return fire. The 100mm D-10S gun of the SU-100 could destroy German medium and heavy tanks at 1,000-1,300m if the side armour was presented.

After defeating the Wehrmacht at Lake Balaton, troops of the 3rd Ukrainian Front moved on to liberate Hungary, southern Czechoslovakia and Austria. The 1st Guards Mechanised Corps with three brigades armed with the SU-100, namely the 382nd Guards, 1453rd and 1821st brigades, participated in all these battles. In addition, the 207th Self-Propelled Artillery Brigade and the SU-100 regiments allocated to the 9th Guards Army were engaged in these operations. SU-100s of the 1st Guards Mechanised Corps took part in the Vienna strategic offensive operation, which resulted in the capture of the Austrian capital.

The SU-100 also participated in the East Prussian strate-

This SU-100 photographed in Prague in May 1945 probably belonged to the 1893rd Self-Propelled Artillery Brigade. Note that the weld seams for the track guards were not parallell to the hull edge, and that a large section of the track guard is missing, as are all but one of the spare links. (Marek Solar)

This SU-100 belonged to the 1289th Self-Propelled Artillery Regiment and was knocked out in the village of Ořechov, Czechoslovakia. One hit is clearly visible on the side of the hull. (Marek Solar)

A burned out SU-100 on Údolní street, Brno, Czechoslovakia.

An SU-100 with the tactical number 740 of the 13th Army of the 1st Ukrainian Front, Sachsen, Sayda region, April 1945. From this view, it is difficult to determine the month of production of this SU-100, but it has typical wartime production features, including the cast front beam, rounded front track guards, one missing, the early D-10S gun, and a double leaf hatch on the commander's cupola.

A Red Army SU-100, Mongolia, 1945. Note the rounded original track guards, "full set" of seven track links bolted to the glacis, and what appears to be planking neatly stowed on the track guard.

gic offensive operation from 13th January to 25th April 1945. SU-100s from the 1207th SAP transferred to the 186th tank brigade and 381st Guards SAP in the composition of the 178th tank brigade.

SU-100s were directly engaged in the final military action of the Second World War in Europe, the assault on Berlin. The 1st Guards Tank Army under the command of Colonel General Mikhail Yefimovich Katukov advancing towards Berlin from the south had within its composition the 11th Guards Tank Corps including the 1454th SAP armed with SU-100s under the command of Guards. Major Piotr Andreevich Melnikov, and the 8th Guards Mechanised Corps, which had in its composition the 400th SAP, also armed with SU-100s, under the command of the Guards Major Alexander Danilovich Fadeev. However, these regiments were severely under establishment unit strength at the beginning of the assault. Only eight SU-100s remained in the 1454th SAP and nine in the 400th SAP. The 1st Guards Tank Army lost eight SU-100 during the operation to capture Berlin, which lasted from 16th April to 2nd May 1945. This relatively small loss of self-propelled guns was due to the use of battle-honed tactics developed specifically for ar-

moured combat in built-up areas. In city blocks, machine gunners moved forward on both sides of the street, concentrating on windows from where Panzerfaust or sniper fire was located. Tanks moved behind the infantry to destroy street barricades and enemy firing points, which were hindering the advance of Red Army infantry. The SAUs went in last, covering the actions of the machine gunners and tanks, while their powerful guns were used to destroy buildings and other fortified points of resistance, which had proven too difficult for the tank guns.

The 2nd Guards Tank Army of the 1st Belorussian front, which also took part in the capture of Berlin, had in its composition the 1415th SAP with seven SU-100s. A total of 18 SU-100 were lost in combat during the storming of Berlin. Ten were destroyed by anti-tank artillery, but only two SU-100s were lost to the "Panzerfaust", so the effect of this Wehrmacht "miracle weapon" was limited with regard to the SU-100 in the last days of the war.

The 1978th SAP of the 71st Mechanised Brigade of the 9th Mechanized Corps* took part in preventing a break out by Wehrmacht troops from a Red Army encirclement in the area of Halbe during the night from 26th to 27th April.

In full, the 1978th SAP of the 71st Mechanised Brigade of the 9th Mechanised Corps of the 3rd Guards Tank Army of the 1st Ukrainian Front.

SU-100s participated in the Soviet Victory Parade in Moscow on 24th June 1945 and continued to be used in parades into the early 1950s. The 100mm D-10S gun was modified for tank use as the D-10T and mounted in the T-54 and later T-55 tanks.

Meanwhile, the 3rd Guards Tank Army of the 1st Ukrainian Front including the 1818th SAP, with six SU-100s in its composition, attacked Berlin from the south west of the city.

The 4th Guards Tank Army of the 1st Belorussian Front moved on Berlin from the south of the city. Within the composition of the 4th Guards Tank Army was the 424th Guards SAP of the 6th Guards Mechanised Corps and the 416th Guards SAP of the 10th Guards Tank Corps - with a total of 120 SU-100s, of which 16 were lost in combat.

Far from Europe, on the other side of the Soviet Union, SU-100s were also used in the war against Japan that began on 8th August 1945. The SU-100s used in the short campaign were delivered all the way from recent service in Germany. The SU-100 armed units consisted of the 208th Brigade (1016th, 1068th, and 1922nd regiments) and the 231st Brigade (1038th and 1051st regiments armed with the SU-100 and the 1022nd regiment armed with the SU-85), all included in the troops of the 6th Guards Tank Army of the Transbaikal Front. There was no serious armoured opposition to the SU-100 in the fighting with the Kwantung army in China, and the SU-100 was not thereby used in its primary anti-tank role. The SU-100s in this theatre were used primarily for the bombardment of Japanese reinforced emplacements and other fortifications.

SU-100s during Red Square parade practice in the Moscow Military District (MVO) in 1946. The prominent stowage box was added to UZTM built SU-100s from November 1945.

An SU-100 during post-war military exercises in the Moscow Military District (MVO), followed by an SU-76M. This SU-100 was produced after November 1945.

Mirko Bayerl, who has for many years researched the battles in Hungary in 1945, uncovered some historical German material about SU-100 deployment in the area of Simontornya (Lake Balaton) during operation "Frühlingserwachen".

"A Soviet tank knocked out by one of our Tigers near the railway station in this battle damaged village", states the original photograph caption by the German war photographer Büschel circa 11th March 1945. The village is Simontornya, Hungary.

On 6th March, the Germans had launched their last major offensive of the war, Operation Frühlingserwachen. For this badly planned operation, which aimed to gain control over Germany's last oil sources near lake Balaton, the last German units of the I and II. SS.Pz Corps along with Heer units were assembled for a last gamble to turn the war. The timing was disastrous, as the Hungarian plains had turned into muddy swamps after the long winter, making mechanised progress difficult. The 1st SS Division (Div.) nevertheless managed to reach the village of Simontornya, whereupon they met stiff resistance from the Soviet defence line including SU-100s from the 208th and 209th Self-Propelled Artillery Brigades (SPAB), which had been formed in December 1944. Each brigade had three self-propelled artillery regiments (SPAR) with approximately 21 SU-100s, some T-34 command tanks and some American Lend-Lease supplied half-tracks.

The brigade commander Colonel Alexander Lukyanov had located the 1953rd SPAR (Major N.Mikhailovich) and their 18 SU-100s north of Simontornya in order to prevent the 1. SS Pz. Div. from reaching the village. The 1951st SPAR had dug in around the village of Saregres to fight off the 1. SS Pz.Div. and the 23rd Panzer Div. while the last regiment was placed at Ozora to stop the 12th SS Pz. Div. A few batteries were also dispatched to Szabadhidveg, west of Ozora, to oppose the 3rd and 4th German Cavalry Divisions.

The 1. SS Pz. Div. met hard resistance when attacking Simontornya, with several tanks being knocked out by the 1953rd SPAR, and were ground to a halt near the Janos Haza Mjr on hill 146 north of the village. Tiger IIs were brought forward to knock out the well dug-in SU-100s. A fierce tank battle at ranges from 1,500-2,000m took place and the SU-100 in the photo below was among the knocked out vehicles.

The Germans lost a Tiger II during this fire-fight, likely the one that knocked out this SU-100. Shortly after, the 1953rd SPAR withdrew over the river Sio and then blew the bridge. However, by doing so they mistakenly cut off one of their batteries, which unit had to fight its way to join the 1951st SPAR at Saregres. They distinguished themselves in the following battle and greatly helped slowing down the attacks from the 23rd Pz. Div. and units from the 1. SS Pz. Div. Eventually, the German forces were able to conquer the village and transfer troops and armour across the river. Meanwhile, the 209th SPAB had built up defence

lines and the German forces could not continue their advance further.

Simultaneously, at Ozora, the 208th SPAB arranged an ambush against the 12. SS. Pz.Div. The Soviets allowed the spearhead of the German forces to reach the bridge over Sio, then hit the first and last vehicles in the column, thereby blocking the bridge. The SU-100 crews displayed tactical brilliance and professionalism in this incident; Four Pz. IVs and a Panther were knocked out in the following battle, and the Germans never managed to gain enough strength for another attempt to cross the bridge.

The SU-100s from the 208th and 209th SPABs, with approximately 100 SU-100s in total clearly had a major role in the failure of Operation Frühlingserwachen. The operation was terminated shortly after and the German units withdrew from the area.

It should be noted that the 207th SPAB protected the flank on another part of the front during the operation. The few Tiger IIs available were the only tanks able to knock out the SU-100 when in dug-in positions. The Germans incorrectly referred to the SU-100s as "Josef Stalin tanks" and German tank veterans recall that what they feared most during the battles in Hungary was the "7.62cm Anti-Tank Gun" nicknamed "Ratsch-Bum" (the 76.2mm ZiS-3) and the 100mm "Josef Stalin" (the SU-100).

Accurately determining the actual losses in the battles of Simontornya and Ozora in difficult as both sides interpreted and classified the losses differently. For instance, the 209th SPAB claimed 14 destroyed Tiger IIs between 9th and 13th March, which would be impossible since the s.SS.Pz.Abt 501 only operated 4-8 such tanks at the time, so the numbers are likely exaggerated and the vehicles misidentified by both combatants in the engagement.

Zoltán Tálosi/Mirko Bayerl

Remnants of an SU-100 from the 209th Self-Propelled Artillery Brigade, dug up in Hungary around 2001. The tactical number 415 is still visible.

(Mirko Bayerl)

Post-War Soviet Service

After the Allied victories in Europe and Japan, the SU-100 was involved in service and combat with the post-war Soviet Army, and also in service with many other nations. In October 1956, SU-100s of the 33rd Guards Mechanised Division, at the time stationed in Romania under the command of General-Major E. I. Obaturov, took part in battles against armed protesters on the streets of Budapest during the suppression of the anti-Soviet uprising in Hungary. During this operation, SU-100 self-propelled guns were used in their tradition role - for the destruction of "enemy" strongholds. A single SU-100 was lost during the street fighting.

A decade later and 500km to the northwest of Budapest, the SU-100 was used by Soviet forces during the "Prague Spring" of 1968 in Czechoslovakia. Self-propelled guns of the 9th and 11th Guards Tank Armies of the Western Group of Forces based in Germany (Group of Soviet Forces Germany) were used during operation "Dunai" (Danube) having been moved from East Germany (GDR) to Czechoslovakia. On this occasion however they did not open fire, and were used as a deterrent only, convincing the "rebels" to remain calm, as it were.

The SU-100 was formally maintained in Soviet Army reserve inventory until as late as 1968, before being finally taken out of service - but then nevertheless kept in long-term stra-

Soviet Army SU-100s on manoeuvres, in 1956. Note the early commander's cupola, desant handrails and webbed roadwheels.

An early production SU-100 in post-war Soviet Army service near Khabarovsk, Soviet Far East Military District, 1955-1956. Note the early webbed roadwheels and desant handrail on the cupola only.

tegic reserve storage. The SU-100 had however one last belated Soviet Army combat role, the following decade, during the Soviet war in Afghanistan. By the beginning of the 1980s the SU-100 was clearly far from a "first line" Soviet armoured vehicle, but in a war where Afghan Mujahedeen had no tanks or armour, and where modern armament and armour were not required, the SU-100 was used for the long-range destruction of fortifications and shelters. The exact number of SU-100s used as part of the officially described "Limited Contingent of Soviet Forces in Afghanistan" is unknown, but a small number were used by the Soviet Army before being transferred to the Afghan Army in the mid 1980s, bringing to an end four decades of service with the Red Army and post-war Soviet Army.

Final Recall

In the 1980s, a new use was found for obsolescent SU-100s - as remote controlled range targets. A total of 121 SU-100s were modified as automatic self-propelled targets by the Bo-

risov Tank Depot Maintenance Shop in 1981, in accordance with an order from the Soviet Defence Minister Marshal D. F. Ustinov to install "teletanki" remote control equipment development by the NIII-38 Scientific-Research Testing Institute of Armoured Fighting Vehicles at Kubinka. These remote controlled self-propelled targets were used during the Warsaw Pact exercise "Zapad-81" held in the Belorussian SSR and during other large exercises conducted during the 1980s. A number of these were also used as targets for T-64 main battle tanks at the Magdeburg training grounds of the Group of Soviet Forces Germany (GSFG) in 1983 and 1984 during the "Soyuz-83," and "Zapad-84" military exercises.

Many Soviet era SU-100s were scrapped in the 1980s and early 1990s, however some were installed as war memorials in the Russian Federation, Ukraine and other former Soviet states. As such the SU-100 is relatively common in museum collections, albeit the SU-100s in museum collections being post-war production SU-100s, and in most cases in Western countries, being specifically SD-100s of Czech origin.

A post-war SU-100 in Soviet Army service, in 1954. Note the later enlarged cupola with single piece hatch and the post-war personal effects storage box.

An SU-100 at speed in the post-war Soviet Turkestan Military District. The SU-100 is wartime production but with post-war modifications. Note the welded patch on the gun mantlet.

The SU-100 has remained an irregular Red Square parade participant to the present day. The variant shown, as paraded on 9th May 1985 and again on 9th May 1990 has the later "starfish" road wheels, infra-red night driving lights, a half-set of tools. (Mikhail Baryatinsky)

An SU-100 crew receiving orders in the immediate post-war era. The vehicle on the left has the later enlarged cupola and a well mangled personnel effects box of the early type. Note the later towing cable set on the vehicle on the right.

The SU-100 in Post-War Foreign Service

The wartime SU-100 remained in Soviet post-war service for many years. It was a much cheaper and simpler combat vehicle to operate than more modern armoured vehicles, particularly for training purposes, and so it had a relatively long "reserve" life in the Soviet Army. The SU-100 was however also a simple and reliable chassis, its 100mm D-10S gun was an excellent and proven design, and was the same armament as used in the T-54 and later T-55 main battle tanks. As such, new types of ammunition developed for these contemporary tanks were also made available for the obsolescent SU-100, which kept the SU-100 current in terms of battlefield potency for several decades, albeit in a reserve status in the Soviet Army. While the SU-100 became a training and reserve status SAU in the Soviet Army, the SU-100 was adopted by the armies of other countries, and saw service in many post-war local and not so local conflicts and wars.

Poland (SU-100)

The People's Army of Poland (Ludowe Wojsko Polskie - LWP) became the First foreign army to receive the Soviet SU-100. The first two SU-100s were delivered to the Polish 46th Self-Propelled Artillery Regiment on 9th May 1945. Poland received a few SU-100s in the early 1950s, as SU-100s were transferred out of Soviet Army service due to the new T-54 tank with the same armament entering Soviet Army service in large quantities. As at 31st December 1954, the LWP had 25 SU-100s in service, which remained in Polish inventory into the 1970s.

Czechoslovakia (SD-100)

Czechoslovakia received only a few original Soviet SU-100s as reference samples, but in 1949 the CKD Sokolovo Locomotive Plant in Prague received a licence from the Soviet Union to produce the T-34-85 and SU-100 in Czechoslovakia. The V-2 diesel engines for these vehicles were produced at the Skoda plant in Plzeň (Pilsen). Czechoslovakian T-34-85 tank production began in 1951, followed in 1953 by the Czech produced version of the Soviet SU-100, which was designated SD-100 (Samohybné Dělo-100mm), with the locally produced D-10S armament being accordingly designated as the 100mm vz. 44S.

A total of 1420* SD-100s were produced from 1953 until production ceased in 1956, of which almost 25% were exported to other Soviet client states. The SD-100 remained in Czechoslovakian service until the early 1970s, after which they were put into long-term storage. With the peaceful partition of Czechoslovakia into the Czech Republic and Slovakia in 1992, the Czechoslovakian inventory of SD-100s was split between the new states.

Some SU-100s were also delivered to the armies of Hungary, Bulgaria, Romania and Albania, with a small number of SU-100s remaining in service in Albania as late as 1995. Soviet built SU-100s were also directly delivered by the Soviet Union to Mongolia.

After the creation of the Warsaw Pact organisation in 1955, the Nationale Volksarmee (NVA) - the National People's Army or East German Army - of the German Democratic Re-

The first two SU-100s were delivered to the 46th Self-Propelled Artillery Regiment of the Polish People's Army (LWP) on the eve of 9th May 1945, with the majority of Soviet built SU-100s delivered to Poland in the very early 1950s. This SAU, with post war upgrades including T-44 type roadwheels and angular hinged mudguards is however the much rarer SU-85M as denoted by the gun mantlet and shorter gun barrel. (Steven J. Zaloga)

This Czech SD-100 was captured by the IDF and is today on display at the IDF Military History Museum in Tel Aviv.

public (GDR) received 23 SU-100s for the 9th Armoured Division (9th NVA Tank Division) where they were used until the beginning of 1960s.

Yugoslavia (M-44)

Yugoslavia was not a member of the Warsaw Pact, but after the death of Stalin in 1953, there was a gradual warming of relationships between Yugoslavia and the Soviet Union in the mid 1950s. After the Belgrade Declaration, signed on 2nd June 1955, during a visit by Nikita Khrushchev to Yugoslavia, the country began to decrease its purchases of Western military equipment. Talks on the purchase of Soviet military technology started on 19th April 1961, with a loan agreement being signed on 4th August the same year. The total cost of Soviet military supply was US $115,912,474 (about US $890 million in current values), with the Yugoslavian government aim being to replace some of its American wartime legacy armoured vehicles with new Soviet hardware.

Talks were initially held with regard to acquiring T-54 M-1951 tanks, MiG-21F-13 jet fighters, surface-to-air missile systems, radar systems and other modern equipment, in which list the SU-100 did not originally figure. However, on 16th May a Yugoslavian delegation in Moscow headed by General Martin Dasović asked about the possibility of purchasing 25 or more SU-100 SPGs if the price was realistic. The Soviet answer was

received on 2nd June, confirming the availability of SU-100s at a unit price of US $54,476 each, US $2,168 for a set of SAU ammunition (33 pieces), and US $8,233 for each spare V-2-34 engine. In addition Yugoslavia was offered the ability to license produce 100mm ammunition locally and to be provided the full set of technical documentation required for SU-100 repairs and capital rebuilds. The Yugoslavians agreed with this offer and contracted to purchase 40 SU-100s from the Soviet Union. In Yugoslavia the SU-100 was known as the M-44.

The new Soviet military equipment was sent to Yugoslavia almost immediately, beginning from the autumn of 1961. The SU-100s were transported by sea in November and December, with 20 SU-100s in each batch, together with the first 20 T-54 tanks. In Yugoslavian service the SU-100 received the new designation M-44 and 4-digit registration numbers of the Yugoslavian People's Army (JNA). Vehicles №0765 and №0766 went initially to the Artillery Training Centre in Zadar (they were later sent to the Nikinci training and testing ground) while №2366 was used for testing ammunition during the 1960s. Other vehicles received registration numbers from 9800 to 9835 and 9861. The 590th Artillery Brigade in Ćupriji in Western Serbia received 24 M-44s to replace their obsolete 57mm (6pdr) guns. Twelve M-44s were sent to the 158th Artillery Brigade in Dakovica, in the south west of Kosovo. The last four were split between the personnel familiarisation and training

---

According to Russian primary sources, Czechoslovakia licence built 1,420 SD-100s over the period 1951-56.

A Yugoslavian SU-100 (M-44) leaving a tank landing craft, 1978. This SU-100 was produced at UZTM before May 1945, with subsequent 1950s upgrades. Note the early D-10S gun installation and commander's cupola with twin leaf hatch.

areas at the Artillery Training Centre in Zadar (two vehicles) and the 1st and 7th Army, which received one each.

The Yugoslav People's Army (JNA) High Command began the reorganisation plan "Drvar-2" in 1964-65, in accordance with which the separate artillery anti-tank brigades changed structure from a battery to a two-regimental composition. Each new brigade received one regiment armed with 18 M-44s and 8 2P27 anti-tank missile launchers on the BRDM chassis, with the other one being armed with 18 ex-U.S. M36 Jackson SPGs and 8 2P26 anti-tank missile launchers mounted on the GAZ-69 light truck chassis.

Although Yugoslavia never joined the Warsaw Pact during the Cold War, it took particular note of the combined Warsaw pact invasion of Czechoslovakia in August 1968, the events spurring a further change in JNA structure. A new mechanised brigade was formed for quick response to any attempt at foreign invasion on Yugoslav soil. The anti-tank battalion of this brigade received all the M-44s from the 590th Artillery Brigade. The anti-tank divisions of the 12th "Proletarian", 36th and 51st motor-mechanised units received six M-44 SPGs and 12 2P27 ATGM vehicles each. These units were reinforced at the beginning of the 1980s when M-44s from other units were col-

Brand new SU-100 self-propelled guns in a storage depot of the ČSR (Czechoslovakian) Army photographed in early 50s. The solid white tactical number 415 can be seen on the vehicle in the centre. Worthy of note are the 200 litre fuel drums placed on the rear engine deck. (Marek Solar)

lected and split between the three mentioned brigades. Each anti-tank division now had a so-called "long" (range) battery of twelve M-44s and an ATGM battery with four 9P133 launch vehicles on the BRDM-2 chassis.

In accordance with JNA standards the M-44 underwent medium repair after 2,500km of running and total rebuild after 5,000km. In full combat readiness, M-44s had 15 HE-Frag and 18 anti-tank rounds of ammunition stowed within each M-44, 40 signal flares for the 26mm flare pistol, 20 fragmentation and 8 smoke grenades. Locally produced 100mm anti-tank rounds could penetrate 185mm of vertical armour at a range of 1,000m

and 156mm at 2,000m. For comparison, imported American 90mm rounds could penetrate 141mm at 500m and 131mm at 1,000m in the same conditions according to Yugoslav sources.

Cumulative ammunition for the 100mm gun appeared in Yugoslavia later in 1960s, which considerably increased the effectiveness of Yugoslavian T-54 tanks and M-44 (SU-100) SPGs. All 40 of the JNAs M-44s remained in service until the outbreak of Yugoslavian Civil War in 1991, most being used in combat in Eastern Slavonia. Vehicles from Đakovica became a part of Srpska Krajina Army. After the 1996 ceasefire they were transported to Sombor in Northern Serbia and most of them

An SU-100 in service in Cuba. This vehicle has typical 1960s upgrades including the stowage box for the MZA-3 electric fuel transfer pump mounted behind the commander's cupola. This SU-100 was built between May and November 1945 (note the direct butt welded glacis armour and lower plates). The vehicle retains the original type commander's cupola which was from November 1945 enlarged and provided with a one piece hatch.

were scrapped in accordance with peace treaty conditions. Only five M-44s survived: two (№9827 and №9834) are located as museum exhibits on the territory of the military base at Kačarevo, Northern Serbia, the three others (№0765, №9824 and №9831) being located at the Nikinci artillery test centre. The last known "operational" use of an M-44 was on 22nd August 2008, when M-44 №9831 was used to test-fire ten domestically produced Balkan Novotech M-63P-2 HE rounds.

Cuba

One very particular end user of the SU-100 was Cuba. During a visit to the Soviet Union by Raul Castro, the Minister of the Revolutionary armed forces of the Republic of Cuba (and younger brother of the famous "El Comandante" Fidel Castro) in July 1960, a communiqué was signed which defined the long-term obligations of the USSR in support of the Cuban Revolution. Among other military equipment delivered to the island were a few dozen T-34-85 medium tanks and SU-100 self-propelled guns. These armoured vehicles were involved in defensive engagements at Playa Girón and Playa Larga in the Bahía de Cochinos on 18th April 1961, fending off beach landings by counter-revolutionary troops disembarked from American ships with the support of American armoured vehicles provided by the United States. The American sponsored landings were unsuccessful and the failed "Bay of Pigs" landings accor-

dingly took their place in military history. A significant number of SU-100s survive today as monuments in Cuba, which also dumped many ex-service SU-100s in the sea where they are today a residence for tropical fish and an unusual attraction for tourist scuba divers.

Asia Pacific

The Soviet Union provided SU-100s to North Korea, however these were supplied after the end of the Korean War in which the T-34-85 had participated. Soviet built SU-100s were delivered to China, where they were radically modernised for service with the Chinese People's Liberation Army (PLA).

In Asia Pacific, SU-100s were delivered to Vietnam in 1973. These SU-100s had undergone 1960s level modernisation and capital repairs. In 1975, some of these SU-100s took part in the "Spring Offensive" by the Vietnam People's Army, which ended with the capture of Saigon.

Middle East & Africa

In the Middle East and Africa, SU-100s (the majority being Czechoslovakian built SD-100s) were delivered to Algeria, Angola, Egypt, Syria and Yemen. SU-100s were also indirectly supplied to Iraq and Morocco via neighbouring countries.

Several hundred Czech built SD-100s were delivered to Egypt in 1953, where they were used during the Suez crisis of 1956. In October 1956 these SPGs were used in combat aga-

A knocked out Egyptian SD-100. (Steven J. Zaloga)

One of several SD-100s knocked out by the 3rd Battalion, British Parachute Regiment (3 Para) in Egypt. One example returned to Great Britain is now on display at the Tank Museum at Bovington, Dorset. (Steven J. Zaloga)

inst the Israelis, advancing on the Sinai Peninsula during the "Kadesh" operation. Four SD-100s from a separate unit of the 53rd Artillery Battery were on 5th November 1956 used in the defence of Port Said against advances by British and French troops, which moved on the city during operation "Musketeer". The SU-100s were as expected inappropriately deployed, resulting in all four SD-100s being destroyed or captured by the British 3rd Battalion of the Parachute Regiment within the 16th Independent Parachute Brigade assigned to the operation in Egypt. The Czech built SD-100 located at the Tank Museum in Bovington was captured during this operation, as is the SD-100 located at the Saumur tank museum in France.

Some years later, during the Arab-Israeli "Six-Day War" of 1967 and again during the "Yom Kippur" war in 1973, Egyptian SU-100s were again used in combat, in both cases against Israeli forces - and again with little success and with heavy losses. As a result of these conflicts, Israeli military museums now have several SD-100s captured in good condition.

The Syrian Army also used SU-100s (SD-100s), which were used in combat against Israel in 1967, and again against Israel in

the above-mentioned 1973 "Yom Kippur" war, in a coalition with Egypt operating in the Golan Heights. These SAUs were used for the direct support of infantry rather than in their designed over-watch role, and with predictable disastrous results.

The Soviet Union supplied T-34-85 tanks and SU-100s directly to Yemen beginning from 1957. Egypt assisted the anti-monarchist coup in Yemen by providing a quantity of their SD-100s in 1962. Their service in Yemen was perhaps the longest of any nation - at least one serviceable SU-100 self-propelled gun remains at present in operation with anti-government Shiite groups in Yemen.

After the break-up of the Warsaw Pact and the Soviet Union, some decommissioned SU-100s and SD-100s were obtained by private collections in Europe and elsewhere, many being the Czech origin SD-100s from users in Eastern Europe rather than Russian built SU-100s. There are a relatively large number of SU-100s mounted on plinths in former Soviet bloc countries, and in museums collections worldwide, reflecting the late war combat service of the SU-100 and its widespread post-war deployment.

Chapter 7

SU-100 description

The SU-100 "medium self-propelled anti-tank unit" was based on the SU-85, with design continuity carried over from the 85mm armed SU-85 self-propelled gun as also produced at UZTM, with both the SU-85 and SU-100 being based on the UZTM production T-34 chassis. 72% of the parts (3,107) were borrowed from the T-34 - including all the running gear and engine compartment components; about 4% (180 parts) were inherited from the SU-122; 7.5% (329 parts) from the SU-85 (mostly the armour plates) and only 16.5% (712 parts) were designed from scratch to install a new 100mm D-10S gun, and in connection with some changes to the fighting compartment and armour strengthening.

The UZTM plant worked in close cooperation with other plants located in the Urals region. The lead designer on all components common with the T-34 tank was Plant №183 located in Nizhny Tagil. Plant №9 of the People's Commissariat of Armaments (NKV) located in Sverdlovsk designed and produced the 100mm D-10S gun (later modified as the D-10SK), with the forgings for the guns being provided to Plant №9 by UZTM which then in turn undertook the final assembly. The later 100mm D-10SK gun was produced at Plant №9 and also at Plant №8.

Plant №50, formerly located within the UZTM plant structure in Sverdlovsk produced the five-speed gearbox, fuel tanks, wheels and some other components. Leningrad Motor Plant №76, which was in late 1941 evacuated to Sverdlovsk, produced the V-2 diesel engines for the SU-100. The Sverdlovsk Tyre Plant and Rubber Products Plant were created on the basis of the "Krasny Rezinschik" and "Kauchuk" plants, evacuated from Kiev and Moscow respectively - together they produced the solid rubber road wheel rims for tank wheels and various gaskets. Solid rubber road wheel rims were also produced at the Omsk Tyre Plant (Plant number №735) and Plant №563 in Nizhny Tagil.

The SAU fighting compartment was welded from hardened to high hardness rolled armour steel plates and consisted of floor, nose and stern parts, sides, wheel and suspension mounting embrasures, the fighting compartment roof sections and engine compartment. The nose of the glacis was wedge-shaped and was formed by two sloping armour plates, welded using a cast beam (and without a beam from May 1945). The upper frontal armoured plate with a thickness of 75mm was located at an angle of 52° - as with the SU-85. The cut-out for the installation of the armament in the upper armoured plate was offset to the right of the longitudinal axis. The mounting arrangement used to install the 100mm D-10S armament was similar to that of the SU-85. The driver-mechanic's hatch was on the left side of the upper glacis plate, and had an armoured cover with two observation devices. Two towing hooks were welded to the upper frontal armour plate, with caps for fuelling the forward two fuel tanks. The 45mm (on early production SU-100s) lower frontal armour was located at an angle of 60°. On the right side of this plate was a milled access hatch to access the crank for the right idler wheel for track tensioning (the retainer crank for the left guide wheel was accessed from within the driver-mechanic's compartment, as with the T-34). The fighting compartment side armour plate was 45mm located at an angle of 20° to the vertical. The fighting compartment rear armour plate was mounted vertically (unlike the SU-85). The fighting compartment roof armour consisted of a single 20mm thick armour plate, in which was mounted an armoured cupola over the gun detent system, a double leaf commander's hatch with panoramic telescope, a loader's double hatch (on early production SU-100s), the commander's cupola and armoured cupolas for the double fans.

The cast commander's sponson and cupola was an asymmetrical oval shape rather than exactly circular when viewed from above, with the armour being up to 90mm over the frontal aspects and up to 40mm at the rear. The cupola had five viewing slits fitted with armoured glass, the location of which was not uniform, and arranged so as to maximise the viewing circle. The fan cupolas mounted on the fighting compartment roof obstructed all-round visibility.

An Mk.4 periscope was mounted in the commander's hatch, which was originally a double-leaf type, which was replaced after the war by a redesigned single cover hatch.

The lower hull, engine and transmission compartments on the SU-100 were identical to the T-34 (76) as produced at UZTM, and not the concurrent T-34-85 then in production at other plants.

The hull side armour behind the tracks was 45mm and above the tracks was 20mm. The rear armour plates were as for the T-34 and SU-85. The upper rear plate was 40mm thick and

Plan view of the SU-100 (late production) hull.

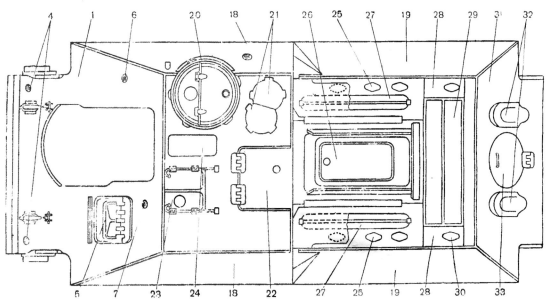

1. Front glacis armour plate.
4. Access to the track tensioning mechanism.
5. Driver-mechanic's hatch armoured cover.
6. Filler cap for the two front fuel tanks.
7. Firing port for firing crew personal weapons.
18. Front side armour plate.
19. Rear side armour plate.
20. Commander's cupola.

21. Double hemispherical armoured housings for the exhaust fans.
22. Gun loader's hatch.
23. Panoramic sight hatch cover.
24. Armoured cupola over the gun recoil system.
25. Oil tank filler cap.
26. Engine compartment hatch.
27. Longitudinal air intake grilles.

28. Engine compartment armoured plates.
29. Engine radiator rear grilles.
30. Filler cap for the rear fuel tank.
31. Upper rear armour plate.
32. Armoured exhaust covers.
33. Hatch to transmission compartment.

Left side view of the SU-100 (early production hull). The armour diagram shows the connection of the front upper and lower armour plates on the late production SU-100, as produced from May 1945.

New hull glacis joint without beam.

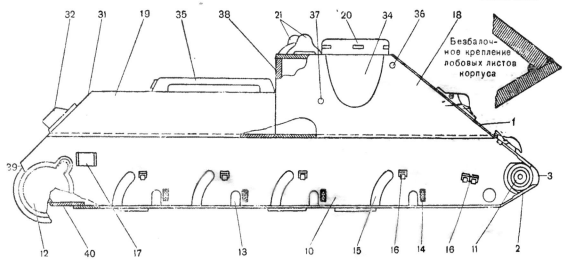

1. Upper front armour plate.
2. Lower front armour plate.
3. Hull front cast beam.
10. Lower side vertical armoured plate.
11. Idler mounting location.
12. Drive sprocket location.
13. Mounting for the axis of the road wheel arms.
14. Road wheel arm stop limiter.
15. Embrasure for road wheel arms trunnion.

16. Rubber stop for road wheel arms.
17. Track "reset" plate.
18. Front side armour plate.
19. Rear sides armour plate.
20. Commander's cupola.
21. Double hemispherical armoured housings for the exhaust fans.
31. Rear upper armour plate.
32. Armoured exhaust covers.

34. Sponson for commander's cupola.
35. Armoured side cover for longitudinal grilles.
36. Radio antenna input.
37. Firing port for firing crew personal weapons.
38. Rear fighting compartment armour plate.
39. Rear middle armour plate.
40. Rear lower armour plate.

located at an angle of 47° 40' to the vertical, the lower rear plate of the same thickness located at an angle of 45°. The standard 550mm diameter round hatch in the upper rear plate gave access for replenishing the gearbox oil and to the ST-700 starter. The two exit windows for the exhaust pipes were provided with protected armoured covers that were bolted to the rear armour plate. The upper armoured plate was folded down on hinges for access, by unscrewing the bolts around the perimeter if necessary for repair of transmission elements such as the gearbox, side clutches or band brakes. Two rear towing hooks were welded to the lower armour plate.

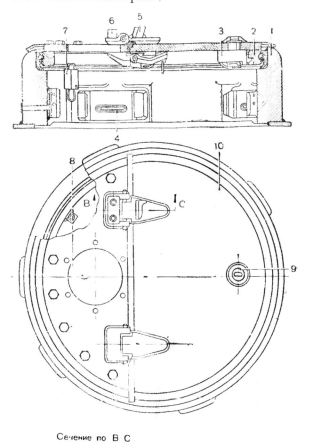

Сечение по В С

Рис. 26. Командирская башенка:
1 — корпус башенки; 2 — подвижный погон; 3 — замок-защёлка; 4 — смотровая щель; 5 — угольник; 6 — резиновый буфер; 7 — стопор; 8 — отверстие для установки смотрового прибора; 9 — отверстие для ключа; 10 — крышка люка; 11 — пружинная защёлка; 12 — торсион

Hatch hinge and torsion bar construction.

The hull floor was assembled from five sheets of armour (on UZTM production SU-100s) with a thickness of 20mm, welded together and with reinforcement plates within the hull. The fifth narrow hull floor plate was called the "lower stern plate" and had a thickness of 40mm.

An emergency hatch, which opened down and to the right, was located on the right side of the hull floor under the commander's seat on the SU-100. It was moved from the standard T-34 location, as on the SU-100 the 100mm ammunition stowage would otherwise obstruct egress). In the middle section of the hull floor, a rectangular hatch was located under

Late type commander's cupola with a single-leaf hatch as produced from November 1945.

1. Commander's cupola turret.
2. Commander's hatch ball race.
3. Hatch lock.
4. Vision slit.
5. Limit stop for hatch leaf in opened position.
6. Rubber stop for hatch leaf in opened position.
7. Hatch rotation latch.
8. Hole for mounting the MK. 4 periscope
9. Keyhole.
10. Commander's hatch.
11. Spring lock.
12. Torsion bar.

The front section of the SU-100 hull floor armour plate. The welded-over bosses that fastened the various internal hardware in the driver-mechanic's compartment are evident.

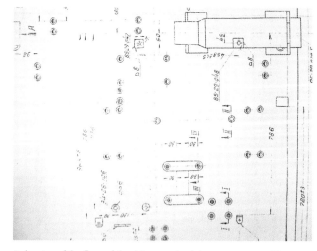

A drawing of the floor of the driver-mechanic's compartment with mounting bolts and rivets clearly evident.

the engine, intended primarily for access to the cooling system drain taps. To the left of this was a drain hole, technically for any water that might get trapped inside the hull. A Bowden cable release was used to drain the cooling system from a valve on the water pump, through a pipe connected to a hole in the hull floor, to the left of the access plate as viewed from above, looking forward. Removal of the plate itself allowed access to the water and oil pumps for maintenance.

Further there is a round "patch" under the engine cooling system fan, the "patch" being lap-welded to the lower armoured plate to ensure sufficient clearance between the bottom plate and the fan impeller. The designers of the T-34 used this unusual engineering solution to prevent potential contact between the centrifugal fan blades and the hull floor if the latter became deformed. At the junction of the fourth and last rear floor plate there was a hatch, used to drain the oil from the transmission (on the T-34 with a four-speed gearbox it was located one the central axis, but with the appearance of a fi-

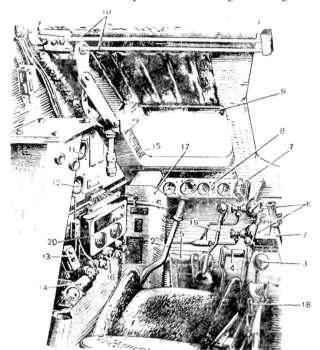

The driver-mechanic's compartment - wartime production SU-100.

1. Driver-mechanic's seat.
2. Side clutch control lever.
3. Accelerator pedal.
4. Brake pedal.
5. Main clutch pedal.
6. Compressed air cylinders for engine starting.
7. Lamp for illuminating the instrument panel.
8. Instrument panel.
9. Observation instrument.
10. Driver-mechanic's hatch torsion bar.
11. Speedometer.
12. Tachometer.
13. Driver-mechanic's telephone box - TPU-3-Bis-F tank intercom telephone system.
14. Engine starter button.
15. Lever stop - driver-mechanic's hatch cover.
16. Horn.
17. Front wheel spring suspension cover.
18. Hand throttle lever.
19. Linkage lever.
20. Electrical instrument panel.

The driver-mechanic's compartment - post-war production SU-100.

1. Lever stop - driver-mechanic's hatch cover.
2. Driver-mechanic's hatch torsion bar.
3. Spring suspension cover - front wheel.
4. Lamp for illuminating the instrument panel.
5. Side clutch control lever.
6. Electrical instrument panel.
7. Linkage lever.
8. Air pump.
9. Battery disconnect switch.
10. Side clutch control lever
11. Compressed air cylinders for engine starting.
12. Ammunition storage under the main armament.
13. Hand throttle lever.
14. Accelerator pedal.
15. Brake pedal.
16. Driver-mechanic's seat.
17. Main clutch pedal.
18. Oil pump start button.
19. Engine start button.
20. Horn signal button.
21. Driver-mechanic's telephone box - TPU-3-Bis-F tank intercom telephone system.
22. Electrical instrument panel.
23. Pressure gauge - compressed air start for the engine.

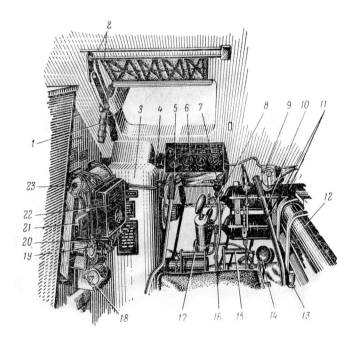

ve-speed transmission (i.e. all of UZTM production) it was off-set 80mm to the right from the central axis. Drain plugs were provided for draining fuel from the fuel tanks if required. By contrast with the T-34-85, due to the grouping of the front fuel tanks being one above the other there was only one drain plug for both tanks, on the right side of the hull floor.

The inclined side armour plate of the engine compartment thickness of 45mm was mounted under an angle of 40° to the

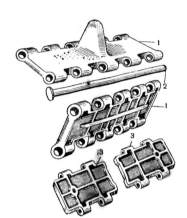

Рис. 210. Траки гусеничной цепи:
1 — траки; 2 — палец траков; 3 — разъёмный трак

Рис. 211. Добавочный почвозацеп (шпора)

vertical. Mounting brackets for the 90 litre external fuel tanks were welded directly to the side armour plates. The roof of the engine compartment consisted of three parts: the side armour plates and the middle section with an armour thickness of 20mm. There were fuel filling ports with armoured covers on each side for refuelling the internal fuel tanks. For oil filler access for fill the oil tanks need open corresponding rectangular hatches in the armoured covers. The central part of the roof of the engine compartment consisted of a convex stamped detail "trough" with a rectangular opening hatch for engine access.

The engine compartment roof side armoured plates each had a small hatch for filling the two central fuel tanks. The armoured side covers were fitted with transverse blinds. The roof of the transmission compartment was covered by a sheet metal cover with a mesh for exhaust heat from the engine compartment. This cover was folded back on its hinges for filling the two rear fuel tanks.

Vehicle and gun ZIP (spare parts) containers were located on the rear right and front left side of the track guards. Brackets were mounted on the left track guard for locating the towing wires, and on the right side for storing 18 track grousers, and a large shovel.

Track links and removable grouser.

1. Track link.
2. Track link pin.
3. Early stamped half-link track link.

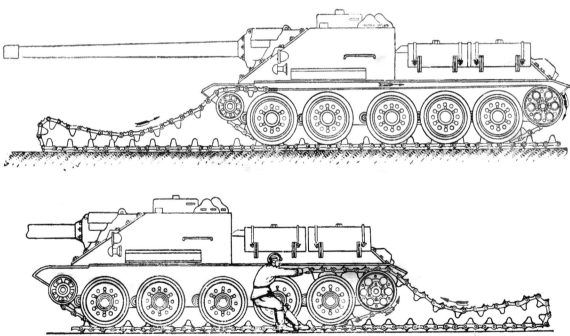

Top: Attaching the track using the drive sprocket and steel tow cable. Bottom: Attaching the track with the drive sprocket only.

The chassis of the SU-100 was borrowed in its entirety from the T-34, with the exception that the steel rod from which the front suspension springs were formed was increased in diameter from 30 to 34mm. On each side of the SU-100 there were five stamped 830mm diameter road wheels fitted with solid rubber rims, each with individual spring suspension. The cast front mounted idler wheel had a diameter of 500mm. The rear drive wheel was 634mm in diameter, with six rollers for engagement with the track link guide horns. Each track consisted of 72 cast steel track links (36 with a guide horn and 36 without),

the tracks being 550mm wide and with a pitch (when new) of 172mm. Early SU-100 track links without the guide horn could also be of stamped construction, formed from two half links. The total track weight was 1,150 kg.

Engine and fuel systems

The engine used in the SU-100 was the same 12-cylinder, four-stroke, high-speed natural pressure liquid-cooled diesel V-2-34 engine as used in the T-34 tank, with a nominal power output of 450hp at 1,750rpm. Operating power was

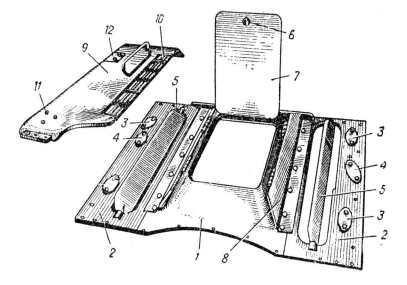

Engine compartment armoured roof.

1. Central convex roof section.
2. Side armoured plates.
3. Armoured covers for the fuel filler caps
4. Armoured covers for the oil filler caps
5. Longitudinal air duct armoured flap
6. Hatch lock.
7. Engine compartment hatch.
8. Additional armoured cover strip.
9. Armoured air duct covers
10. Grille in the armoured side cover above oil cooler.
11. Bolt boss for MDSh smoke drum brackets (post-war upgrade 1960).
12. Armoured hatch cover for the oil filler cap.

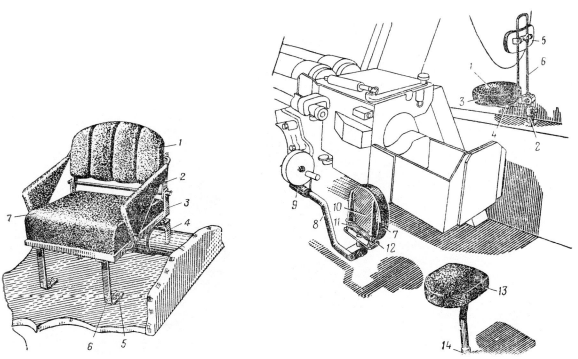

SU-100 crew seats. Left: driver-mechanic's seat. Right: gunner's seat (7), gun loader's seat (13) and commander's seat (1).

400hp at 1,700rpm, with a maximum power output of 500hp at 1,800rpm. A "multi-cyclone" air purifier was used to supply clean air to the cylinders of the diesel engine. The engine was started by means of a ST-700 electric starter with a capacity of 15hp, or if required, by compressed air, for which two cylinders were placed in the front of the driver-mechanic's compartment.

The V-2-34 engine ran on "DT" (diesel) fuel, but could also run on Brand "E" gas oil. The main fuel supply was located in six internal fuel tanks with a total capacity of 400 litres: rear tanks on the right and left sides (two tanks on each side) each with a capacity of 120 litres, plus two front tanks with a total capacity of 160 litres. The fuel was supplied to the engine by an

NK-1 fuel pump. Four removable 90-litre external cylindrical tanks were mounted on the sides of the engine compartment, but these were not connected to the fuel system and acted only as reserve canisters. One of the external tanks was often used for engine lubricating oil. If required, two more additional external fuel tanks could be mounted on the smoke brackets.

Two additional external fuel tanks each with a capacity of 60 litres could be installed on the MDSh or BDSh smoke canister mounting-brackets if required to extend range. The lubrication system was pressurised via a three section oil pump, with the capacity of the two oil tanks being 80 litres of oil, grade MK in summer or grade MZ in winter.

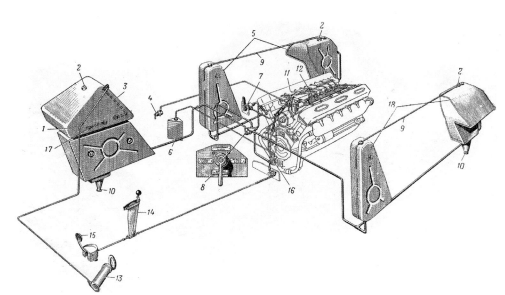

The fuel system.

1. Front fuel tanks group.
2. Fuel filling line cap.
3, 9. Air lines.
4. Drain valve.
5. Right fuel tank group.
6. Drain tank.
7. Hand fuel pump.
8. Fuel distribution valve.
9. Drain valve sumps.
10. Drain valve sumps.
11. Fuel filter.
12. Fuel pump.
13. Hand air pump.
14. Throttle lever.
15. Accelerator pedal.
16. Fuel pump.
17. Fuel tank connection line.
18. Left fuel tank group.

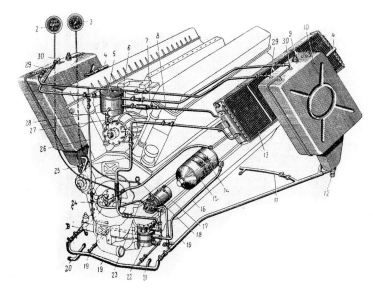

Post-war upgrade oil lubrication system (from 1955).

1. Starboard oil tank.
2. Oil thermometer.
3. Oil pressure gauge.
4. Line from heat exchanger.
5. Balancing reservoir.
6, 26. Drainage pipeline.
7. Lines from the oil tanks to balancing reservoir.
8. Lines from the oil cooler to balancing reservoir.
9. Filling line cap.
10. Left oil tank.
11. Connecting line for draining coolant.
12. Sump oil drain valve.
13. Oil cooler.
14. Lines from oil filter to main feed line.
15. Oil filter.
16. Lines from the oil pump to oil filter.

17. MZN-2 oil priming pump.
18. Pressure gauge sensor.
19. Heated oil lines.
20. Hot liquid line from heater.
21. Line for temporary rubber hoses of the oil heating system.
22. Engine oil pump.
23. Lines from oil priming pump.
24. Thermometer sensor.
25. Lines from oil pump to oil cooler.
27. Lines for oil cooler disconnection.
28. Shut-off valve housing.
29, 30. Oil lines.

This is a wartime specification V-2 engine as used in the SU-100 being overhauled at the Kharkhov Tank Repair Plant in the 1950s. Note the camshaft covers without inspection plates. (Sergei Popsuevich)

The SU-100 used the same V-2 engine and transmission as the T-34 but with some changes to the fuel and cooling systems. This is a post-war V-2 engine mounted in a T-34-85. The installation is generally as for the wartime SU-100 but note that wartime production V-2 engines did not have the six inspection plates on the camshaft covers (for inspecting the injectors). Note also the later VTI-3 air filters. (Peter Plume)

The cooling system was a liquid closed loop forced circulation type. On both sides of the engine were mounted two inclined tubular type radiators with a total capacity of 95 litres. Air was drawn through the radiators by a centrifugal fan, bolted to the engine flywheel. The flow of cooling air entered through the lateral longitudinal louvres and out through the louvres above the transmission compartment at the rear. The cooling water pump circulation pump was mounted on the lower half of the crankcase.

Transmission

The transmission the SU-100 did not differ from later T-34 tanks, and consisted of a multi-disc main clutch dry friction, 5-speed manual transmission with constant-mesh gears, a multi-disc clutch, single stage final drives and variable band brakes. The gearbox and the clutch were controlled from the driver-mechanic's seat through a system of control rod linkages.

The single-stage, step-down gear reducer final drives, were affixed by bolts to the hull side. The drives increased torque to the drive wheels by a multiple factor of 5.7. Two blanking bolts for filling and for draining used oil were located in the each of the final drive crankcases.

Electrical system

The electrical equipment was operated via single-wire circuit with voltage 12v and 24v. Electrical energy was provided by a GT-4563-A generator producing 1kW at 24-volt, and four 6STEh-128 12-volt batteries (two on each side of the engine) with a capacity of 128 Ah each. The 24-volt system was linked to the ST-700 starter and engine start relay, the two MV-12 fan ventilator motors providing ventilation for the crew compartment, the electric trigger action for the gun and the heater for the protective glass of the main sight. The 12-volt system was used for external and internal lighting, the VG-4 signal horn, the electrical igniter for the smoke canisters, and the intercom communication system. The radio worked on both 12v and 24v.

Communications

The early production SU-100 had short-wave simplex 9-PM or 9-RS transmitter/receiver team with an antenna height from 1 to 4 metres, with each 1-metre joint increasing the radio range by about 5km. With a single section 1 metre antenna and the SU-100 stationary, radio transmission range was up to 5km, reducing to 3km on the move. With a full 4 metre antenna, communication at halt was up to 25km, reducing to 18km on the move. The antenna could be rotated to the rear by means of a lever located near to the commander's seat. The radio was mounted in a single combined block consisting of transmitter, RU-45A transformer and receiver RSI-4T (i.e a "fighter aircraft" set in tank configuration), located in front of the commander on a steel shelf, installed on the second right suspension casing. A TPU-3-Bis-F internal intercom was fitted for use by three of the crew (the loader was excluded).

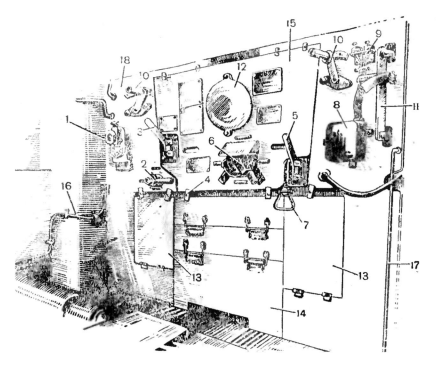

The bulkhead between the fighting compartment and engine compartment (SU-100 - early post-war production).

1. Battery disconnect switch.
2. Fuel distribution valve.
3. Manual fuel pump.
4. Rotary latch.
5. Manual oil pump.
6. Oil distribution valve.
7. Water drain cock / water pump control arm.
8. Electrical fuses for batteries.
9. Smoke cannister control panel.
10. Actuator lever - longitudinal louvres.
11. Actuator lever - rear louvres.
12. Round access hatch. Perhaps related to the NK-1 high pressure fuel pump but not denoted in Soviet manuals.
13. Removable panel to access the batteries.
14. Lower removable panel.
15. Upper removable panel.
16, 17. Fuel line.
18. Bulkhead.

Armament

The initial wartime armament of the SU-100 consisted of a 100mm D-10S (M-1944) gun with a barrel length of 56 calibres and a semi-automatic breech. The D-10S was replaced by the D-10SK post-war. Total weight of the gun was 1,435kg. The gun had a total traverse of 16°, maximum gun depression of -3° and maximum elevation of +20°. The maximum gun recoil was 570mm. The main trigger was electric, with a secondary mechanical trigger. For direct fire, the SU-100 was provided with a TSh-19 articulated telescopic sight, and for firing from concealed positions - a lateral level and panorama sight, with 3.7x magnification and a field of view of 10°. The 100mm gun had a practical rate of fire of 5-6 rounds per minute.

The gun was installed within a large and complex shaped fixed mantlet attached to the frontal armour of the fighting compartment. The mantlet was mounted to the glacis with bolts, for which purpose the mantlet mask was sculpted to allow access to the bolt heads with a pneumatic power tool. A moveable armoured gun mantlet protected the gun externally.

The ammunition complement was 33 rounds, located in the fighting compartment. The rounds were stowed as follows: Left side racks (6), between the spring suspension covers, left side (8), near bulkhead between fighting compartment and engine compartment (8), near right middle cover of the spring suspension (1), in the stowage in the bow of the SU-100 under the gun (8), on the floor of the fighting compartment on the shelves (2).

In addition, in a special container on the floor near the

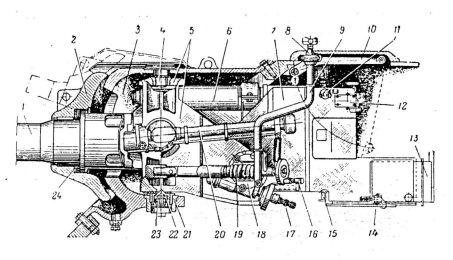

Fighting Compartment and Main Armament.

100mm D-10S Main Armament.
(wartime production)

1. Gun barrel.
2. Gun mantlet.
3. Fixed mantlet armour.
4. Upper gun trunnion.
5. Gun carriage.
6. Recoil mechanism.
7. Stationary section - armament recoil guard.
8. Panoramic sight
9. Extension bracket for Goerz type panoramic sight.
10. Bracket for gun in stowed position.
11. Arc clinometer.
12. VS-11 locking device.
13. Retractable section - armament recoil guard.
14. Terminal switch guard.
15. Firing trigger mechanism.
16. Flywheel - gun horizontal laying mechanism.
17. Flywheel - gun vertical laying mechanism.
18. Housing - gun vertical laying mechanism.
19. Protective housing - gun horisontal laying mechanism.
20. TSh-19 gun sight.
21. Lower gun trunnion.
22. Ball bearing race.
23. Cup lockwashers.
24. Shock absorber.

100mm D-10SK Main Armament
(post-war production)

1. Gun breech
2. The gun commander's (i.e. the Red Army description of the gunner's position) seat.
3. Breech block guard.
4. Firing trigger mechanism.
5. VS-11 locking device.
6. Inclinometer (side level).
7. The gun vertical laying mechanism.
8. Flywheel - gun vertical laying mechanism.
9. Flywheel - gun horizontal laying mechanism.
10. Extension bracket for Goerz type panoramic sight.
11. Gun travel lock.
12. 9-RS radio station.
13. Radio antenna rotation lever.
14. Commander's cupola periscopes
15. Commander's cupola.
16. Commander's seat.

right front spring suspension cover were kept four RPG-40 anti-tank grenades, twelve F-1 defensive grenades were located in a drawer under the driver-mechanic's seat, and twelve F-1 grenades located on the racks above the vertical stowage of rounds on the right side. Also on the right side of the fighting compartment near the commander's seat were located two 7.62-mm PPSh sub-machine guns. Ten drum magazines for the PPSh - on the shelves above the right middle spring suspension cover, and another ten located in three bags behind the right middle spring suspension cover.

The SU-100 was provided with six types of rounds:
• УБР-412 (UBR-412) - unitary round with BR-412 armour-piercing arrowhead projectile and MD-8 fuse;
• УБР-412Б (UBR-412B) - unitary round with BR-412B armour-piercing tracer projectile and MD-8 fuse;
• УО-412 (UO-412) - unitary round with O-412 fragmentation naval projectile and RGM fuse;
• УОФ-412 (UOF-412) - unitary round with OF-412 high-explosive fragmentation projectile and RGM fuse;
• УОФ-412У (UOF-412У) - unitary round with a high-explosive fragmentation projectile OF 412, reduced charge and RGM fuse;
• УД-412 (UD-412) - unitary smoke round weight 30.1 kg with RGM, RGM-6 or V-429 fuses.

Post-war three new types of ammunition rounds appeared:
• УД-412У (UD-412U) - unitary smoke round weight 30.1 kg with V-429 fuse;
• УБР-421Д (UBR-421D) - unitary round with BR-412D armour-piercing tracer armour-piercing ballistic projectile;
• УБК9 (UBK-9) - unitary cartridge with a hollow-charge BK5M projectile.

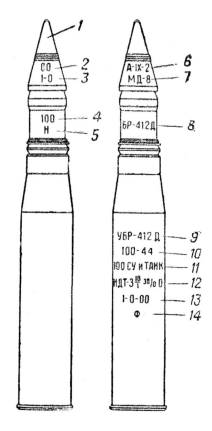

Example of 100mm artillery round marking - the 53-BR-412D armour-piercing tracer round (taken into service 1953).

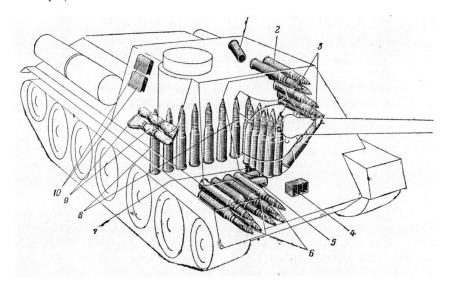

SU-100 ammunition stowage - post-war upgrade.

1. Cartridge with propellant powder.
2. Six rounds stowed on the left side of fighting compartment.
3. Eight rounds stowed near the left vertical side of fighting compartment and another round on the cover of the spring suspension of the left front wheel.
4. Stowage for 12 F-1 hand-grenades.
5. Two rounds stowed on the floor of fighting compartment under the gun.
6. Eight rounds stowed in the bow of the SU-100.
7. Stowage for eight F-1 hand-grenades.
8. Eight rounds stowed near the bulkhead between the fighting compartment and the engine compartment.
9. Stowage for two AK-47 Kalashnikov assault rifles on the right side of fighting compartment.
10. Stowage for two pouches with five magazines in each.

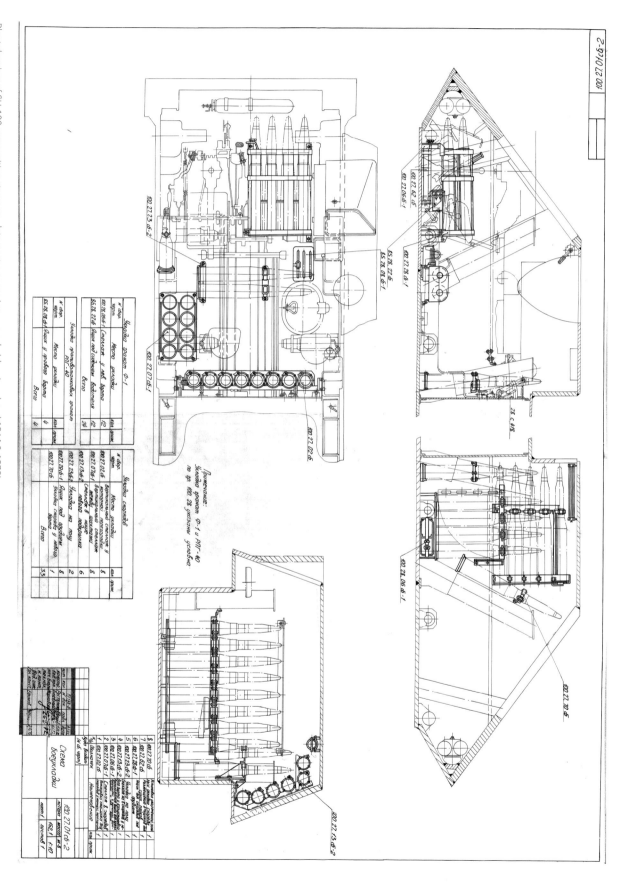

Plant drawing of SU-100 ammunition stowage – late post-war service upgrade (drawing dated 1964 & 1972).

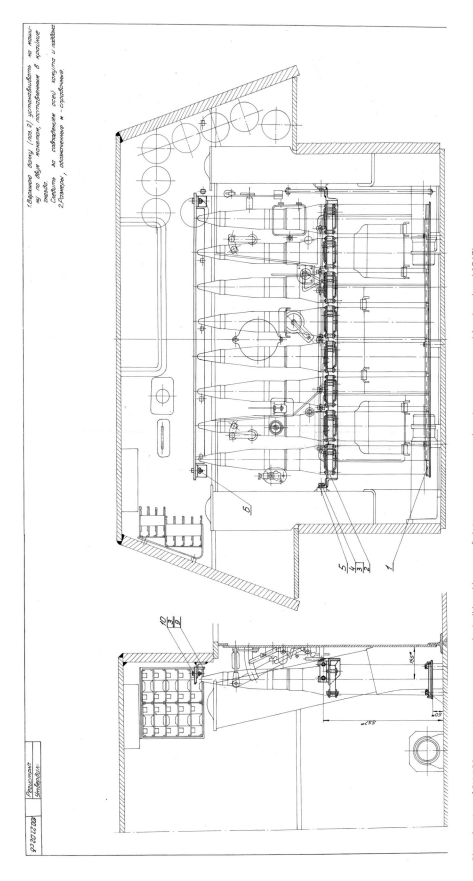

Plant drawing of SU-100 ammunition stowage near the bulkhead between fighting compartment and engine compartment (drawing dated 1967).

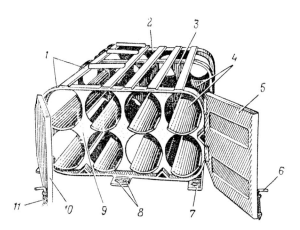

Eight rounds as stowed in the hull front of the SU-100.

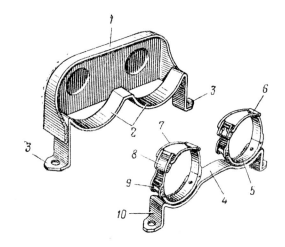

Two rounds stowed on the fighting compartment floor under the gun.

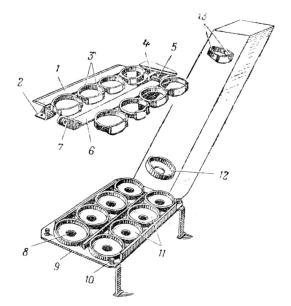

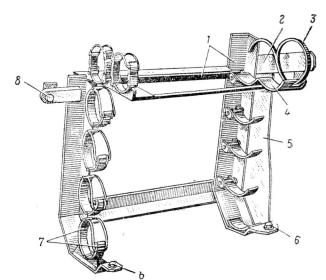

Above: Eight rounds stowed near the left side of fighting compartment plus one round on the cover of the spring suspension of the left front wheel. Six rounds stowed on the left side of fighting compartment.

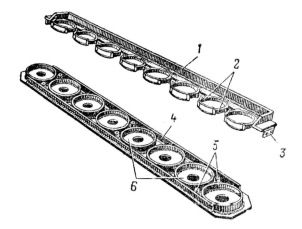

Eight rounds stowed near the bulkhead between the fighting and engine compartments.

SU-100, UZTM Production
- Late 1944

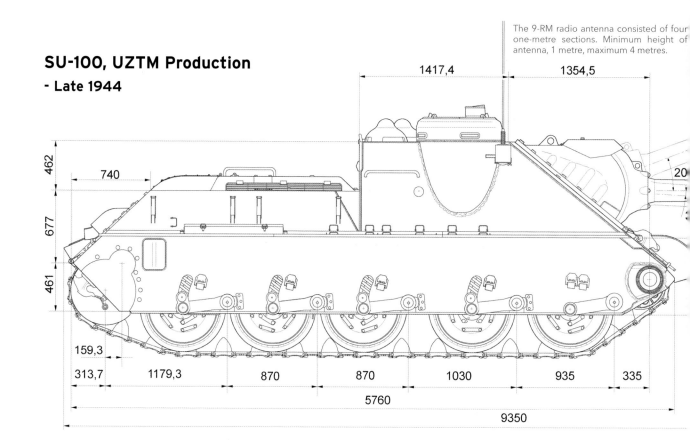

The 9-RM radio antenna consisted of four one-metre sections. Minimum height of antenna, 1 metre, maximum 4 metres.

1417,4   1354,5

462
677
461

740

159,3
313,7   1179,3   870   870   1030   935   335

5760

9350

0   1   2   3м

M 1:35

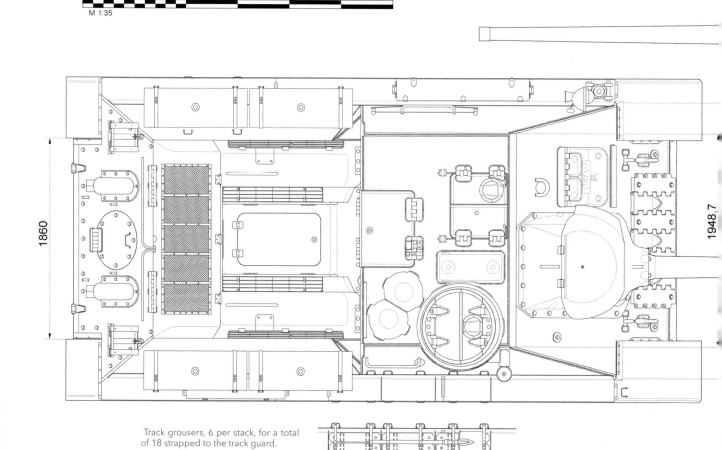

1860

1948,7

Track grousers, 6 per stack, for a total of 18 strapped to the track guard.

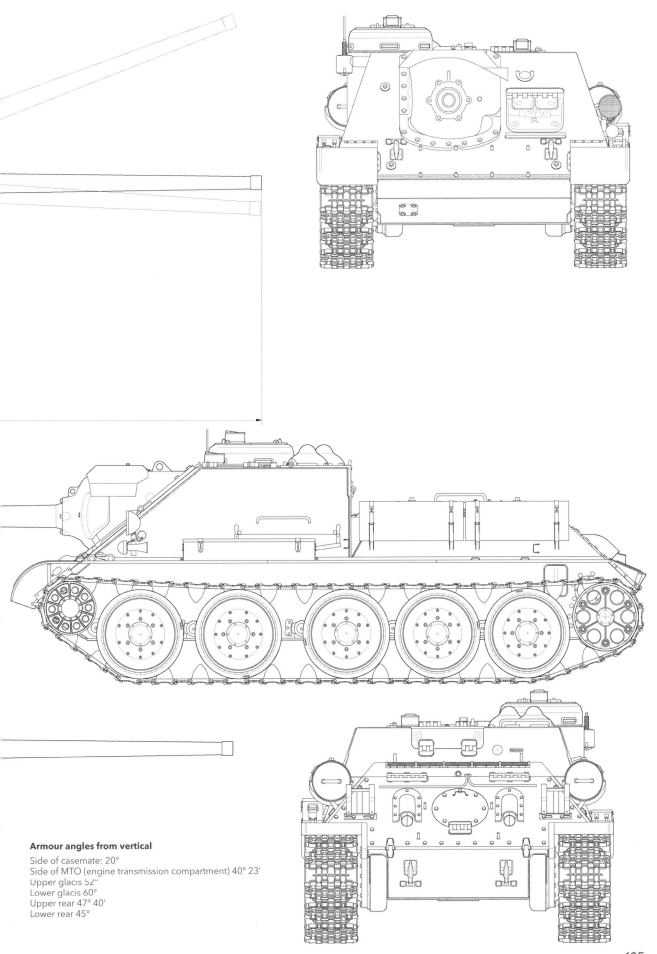

Armour angles from vertical

Side of casemate: 20°
Side of MTO (engine transmission compartment) 40° 23'
Upper glacis 52°
Lower glacis 60°
Upper rear 47° 40'
Lower rear 45°

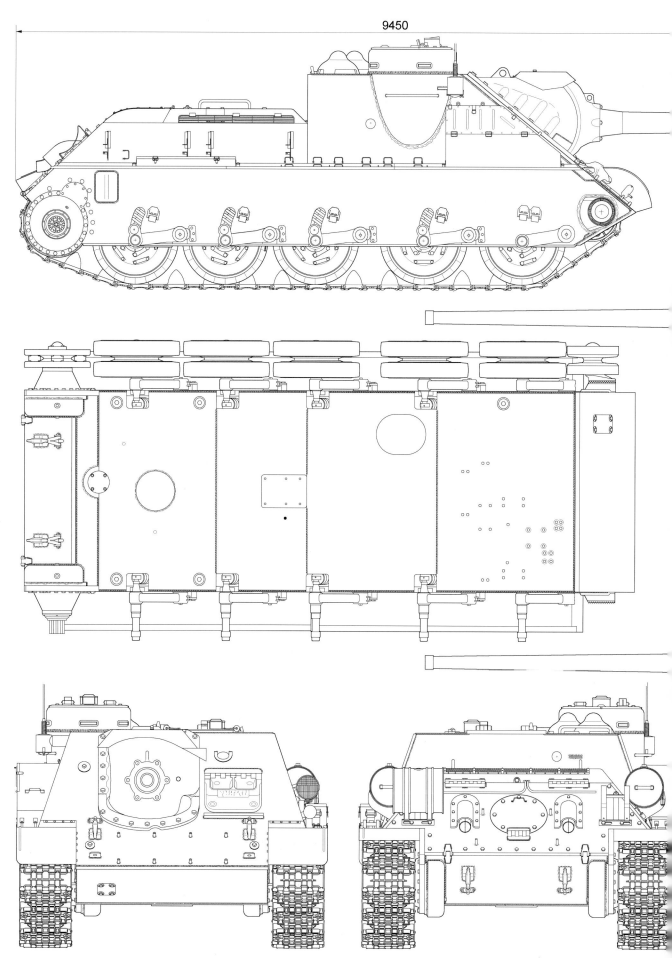

9450

SU-100, UZTM Production
- December 1945

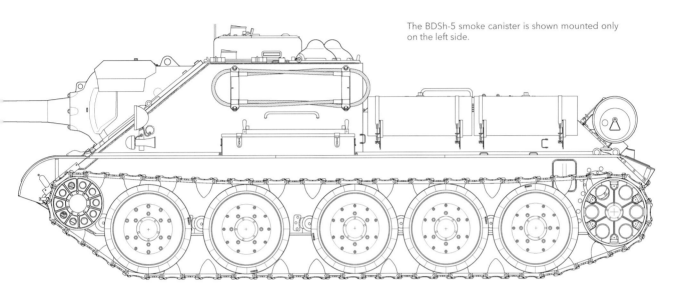

The BDSh-5 smoke canister is shown mounted only on the left side.

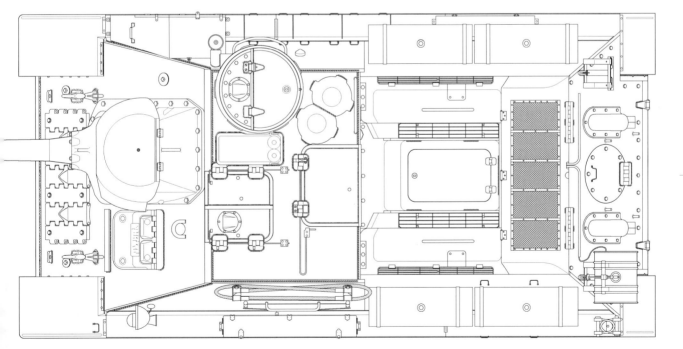

The stowage arrangement for the longer 6.5 metre tow cable is not shown.

M 1:35

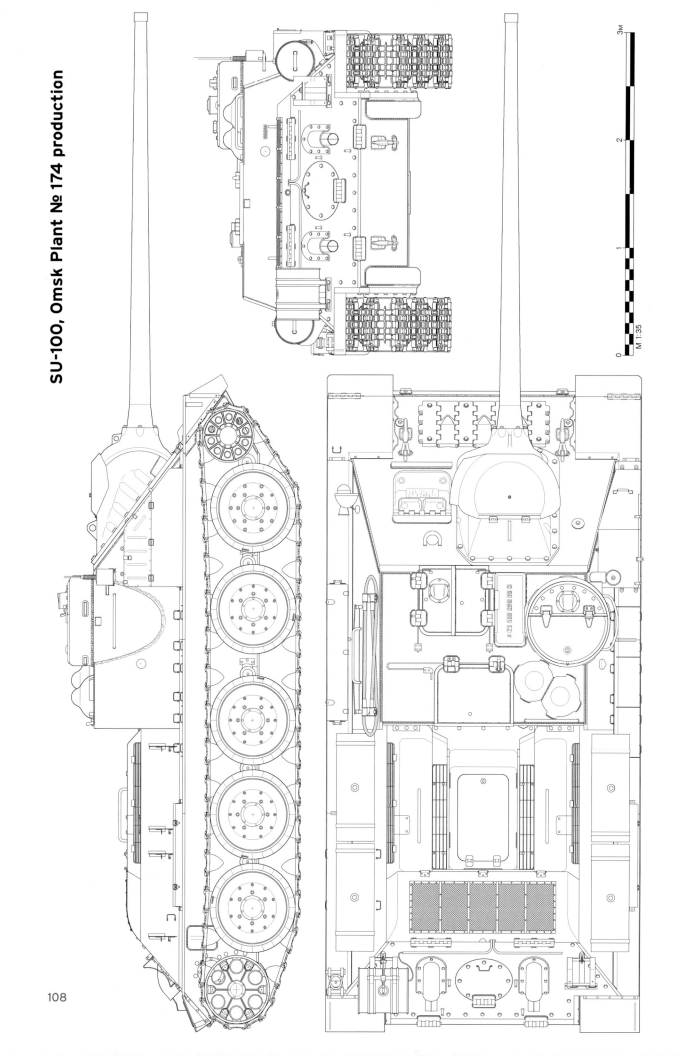

SU-100, Omsk Plant № 174 production

M 1:35

Tactical-Technical Characteristics (TTKhs) of the SU-100 Medium Self-Propelled Gun - Initial 1944 production

Combat weight: 31.6 metric tonnes

Dimensions (mm)
Length with gun: 9450
Width: 3000
Height: 2245
Ground clearance: 350

Armament
Armament 100mm gun D-10S
Ammunition complement: 33 rounds

Armour (mm)
Gun mantlet: 110
Forward upper armoured plate: 75
Forward lower armoured plate: 45
Casemate sides: 45
Rear armoured plates: 40
Hull floor: 20
Hull roof: 20

Engine
V-2-34, 4-stroke, V-12-cylinder diesel engine developing 500hp

Performance
Maximum road speed: 50km/h
Road range: 310km
Road range, with additional fuel tanks: 500km
Fording: 1.3m
Vertical wall: 0.7m
Trench: 2.50m
Angle of approach: up to 35°
Allowable lateral roll, deg. up to 25°

Tracks: 550mm wide, pitch 172mm (new). 72 links per track.

Communications
9RM (later 9RS)
TPU-3 intercom

Crew: 4

Soviet diagrams showing 100mm unitary rounds, marked with their technical characteristics, and wooden transport box stowage arrangement.

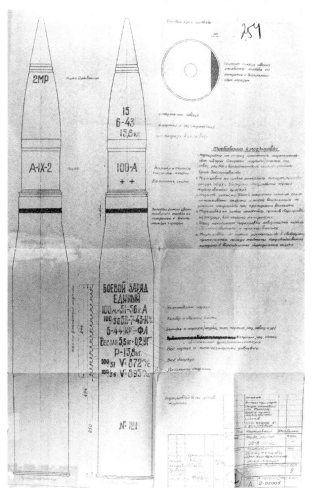
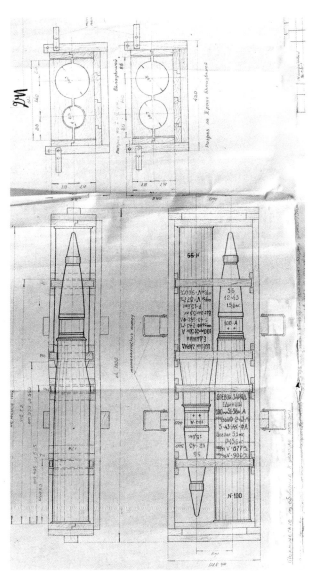

Chapter 8

The Next Generation SU-100

As the SU-100 was being prepared for series production, another more powerful variant was developed to prototype stage on the SU-100 medium chassis, the SU-122P (P - Pushechnaya - tank gun), armed with a 122mm D-25S tank gun developed by Plant N°9. The 122mm D-25S was a modification of the 122mm D-25T as used in the IS-122 / IS-2 heavy tank, adapted for use in medium self-propelled gun mountings, effectively recreating the design principles behind the SU-D-25 self-propelled gun project of 1944.

SU-122P Self-Propelled Gun Prototype

The prototype SU-122P, built on the SU-100 chassis and armed with a 122mm D-25S gun with double baffle muzzle brake and a 26 round ammunition complement, was completed in September 1944. The SU-122P was immediately sub-jected to plant and state trials and was accepted for service with the Red Army. The 122mm D-25S gun did not however offer any particular advantages over the 100mm D-10S in the anti-tank role, and although the 122mm HE-Frag round was a powerful general-purpose shell type, the 122mm D-25S mounted in the SU-100 chassis had a lower rate of fire and a smaller ammunition complement by comparison with the SU-100 mounting the 100mm D-10S. The significant recoil of the 122mm D-25S also prevented accurate fire on the move, while the long barrel length of both the 100mm D-10S and the 122mm D-25S was a concern when crossing uneven terrain and in potential street fighting. Although the 122mm D-25S was not ultimately installed in the SU-122P as a series production SAU, it was however successfully installed in the IS based ISU-122S.

The SU-122P prototype outside the UZTM plant in the autumn of 1944. The distinctive 122mm D-25S gun and mantlet changes are evident, but otherwise the SU-122P is identical to the SU-100. Note however the significantly increased glacis armour. (Mikhail Svirin)

The same SU-122P prototype outside the UZTM plant. Though a potent weapon, the 122mm D-25S gun offered no particular advantage over the 100mm D-10S gun of the SU-100 in the anti-tank role, and mounted in the SU-100 casemate hull also had a slower rate of fire and a reduced ammunition complement. Thought accepted for service, the SU-122P did not enter series production. (Mikhail Svirin)

The SU-122P prototype, armed with the 122mm D-25S gun outside the UZTM administration buildings. (Vyacheslav Belogrud)

The SU-122P during plant trials, demonstrating that the vehicle inevitably suffered from the same difficulties in rough terrain as the SU-100. (Vyacheslav Belogrud)

An SU-100 during the same winter trials at UZTM against the SU-122P. The operating difficulties related to the barrel length had been an accepted compromise when the SU-100 was approved for production.

SU-101 and SU-102 "Uralmash-1" Self-Propelled Guns

In accordance with NKTP Order №625 dated 26th October 1944, Uralmash was instructed to develop potential replacements for the SU-100, which had at the time only just entered production. The plant was instructed to develop production drawings and manufacture trial samples of two alternatives, the SU-100-M-2 and the SU-122-44. The latter was dropped in December 1944, as the vehicle length and combat weight were deemed excessive, though the design would be revived post-war as the SU-122-54.

The SU-100-M-2 was developed further, featuring a rear mounted and more compact fighting compartment with additional armour over the frontal aspects, while remaining within the weight classification for a medium SAU. Development work continued under the direction of B.G. Muzrukov. In January 1945, Narkomtankprom (NKTP) sent a special commission to the Uralmash plant to review the development of the SU-100-M-2 and give comments and recommendations. At the be-

ginning of March 1945 the final plans for the new SAU were presented to NKTP and to the Military Council of Armoured and Mechanical Forces of the Red Army (GABTU). NKTP Order №107 dated 7th March 1945 approved the production of a prototype of the new SAU with a rear mounted fighting compartment and front mounted engine and transmission, with the completion date set as 1st May 1945. The entirely indigenous Uralmash design was designated "Uralmash-1", with development of the prototypes under the overall supervision of L. I. Gorlitsky.

Two trial prototypes of the "Uralmash-1" were completed at Uralmash during March-April 1945. One was armed with a 100mm D-10S gun and was given the designation SU-101. The other was armed with a 122mm D-25S gun and was developed under the index SU-102. The two prototypes and another armoured hull built for artillery range proving trials were completed as the Second World War in Europe was in its final days. The layout of the "Uralmash-1" in both versions provided for a more compact overall design, and negated the main concern

The SU-101, armed with the same 100mm D-10S gun as the SU-100, and the related SU-102, armed with the same 122mm D-25S gun as the SU-122P, were a radical repackaging of the SU-100, eliminating the gun overhang and providing batter crew working conditions and protection.

The SU-101 was a complete reconfiguration of the SU-101, with the casemate mounted at the rear providing better crew conditions while the crew was also protected by the frontal armour and the MTO (motor-transmission) compartment.

The reversed chassis layout is clearly evident in this view, providing several operational benefits, not least a lack of gun barrel overhang. The SU-101 and SU-102 "Uralmash-1" prototypes were also provided with a 12.7mm DShKM anti-aircraft machine gun. (Vyacheslav Belogrud)

with the SU-100 manoeuvring on uneven terrain - namely the barrel length projecting far in front of the hull. The smaller, more compact design also gave the vehicle better overall armour protection, while the crew had a far better chance of survival in the event of an emergency, as they could exit the vehicle through the hatch located in the rear of the hull under cover of the frontal armour.

The results of firing tests on the armoured hull manufactured for the purpose were impressive. The "Uralmash-1" armoured superstructure provided better protection than all Soviet tanks and SAUs then in service, including the IS-2 and the ISU-152. The load distribution on the suspension and running gear was also even, which reduced the severe and uneven wear on

the front suspension that affected the SU-100. The rear mounted fighting compartment also provided the "Uralmash-1" with the option to install more powerful armament with a potentially longer barrel without manoeuvrability concerns.

The fate of the "Uralmash-1" was decided with the end of the war rather than on any technical merit or lack thereof. With the cessation of hostilities, the size of the Red Army was greatly reduced. There were already large numbers of SAUs in service, and the new T-54 medium/main battle tank was under development, armed with the same 100mm D-10 series gun as the SU-101. For these reasons, all further development work on the "Uralmash-1" vehicles was cancelled.

The SU-101 during plant trials against the SU-100. The reconfiguration was drastic, and the resulting vehicle had a higher profile, but from a gun crew and driver-mechanic perspective the SU-101 provided many significant advantages. (Vyacheslav Belogrud)

Chapter 9

SU-100 Walkaround

The SU-100 located at the Museum of Russian Military History at Padikovo, which has been restored back to running condition, is an example of the SU-100 where the history has been researched and is known. The SU-100 (Serial №711977) was built at UZTM in August 1945 and originally fitted with a 100mm D-10SK gun as fitted to all new build SU-100s at the plant from June 1945, and retrofitted to service SU-100s during capital rebuild.

The SU-100 today located at Padikovo is a good example of how the original specification and detail appearance of an ex-works new production armoured vehicle can change over time.

The SU-100 at the Padikovo museum underwent two capital rebuilds, in the 1950s and 1960s, but does not however have all of the modernisation features common to Soviet 1950s upgrades, no GST-49 convoy lights for example being fitted. The SU-100 also underwent modernisation in the1960s, but again has some omissions and some non-standard features from that period.

The container for the electric MZA-3 refuelling pump fitted on late production SU-100s was normally mounted on the right side of the fighting compartment casemate wall, behind the commander's cupola sponson, for which purpose the original "desant forces" handrail was removed. On the Padikovo

museum SU-100, the housing is fitted on the left side as more commonly seen on modernised T-34-85 tanks, but the right side grab handle has nevertheless been removed.

In all likelihood this particular SU-100 spent most of its post-war Soviet Army service in long-term strategic storage, with typical periodic rotation to prevent seizure of mechanical components. The SU-100 was later exported to Bulgaria, apparently sometime in the mid 1960s, as the vehicle does not have any of the common early 1970s Soviet upgrade features.

The SU-100 was located and restored in Bulgaria before being recently returned to the Russian Federation. There remain some incorrect restoration nuances related to restoring it back to a "correct" wartime configuration. The current FG-122 headlight and FG-105 lens combination was never used on armoured vehicles and the signal horn is not a correct military type. The wheel hubs with a central bolt-plugged lubrication point are also a post-war only feature. The attachment points for the (now removed) crew personal effects stowage box on the right side need to be removed for a "correct" wartime appearance, while the radio antenna pot is also a post-war type. There are many other details that need removed to backdate the SU-100 to a genuine wartime specification, which the Padikovo museum plans to do in the near future.

The SU-100 at Padikovo is in running order and has been partly restored back to wartime configuration. (Andrey Aksenov)

GENERAL LAYOUT

The SU-100 at Padikovo was exported to Bulgaria from which it was recently returned after partial restoration. Note the attention to detail such as the correct manufacturing plant specification track grouser stowage arrangement. (Andrey Aksenov)

Front and rear views of the Padikovo Museum's SU-100 almost entirely restored back to World War Two specification but with some post-war features still currently retained. (Andrey Aksenov)

The SU-100 in the (now fully enclosed) tank exhibition hanger. The SU-100 at Padikovo is in fully operational condition. The flags are reproductions of the flag flown over the Reichstag in the final days of World War Two.

All "walkaround" photographs of the SU-100 at the Museum of Russian Military History at Padikovo are courtesy of Andrey Aksenov.

COMMANDER'S CUPOLA

The commanders cupola producsed by UZTM until November 1944.

The commander's two-piece hatch - rear view.

The commander's two-piece hatch - overhead view.

Note the distinct ledge between the sponson and the commander's cupola.

The commander's sponson and cupola.

The commander's hatch is offset to the rear of the cupola, with the frontal armour being greater than the rear - up to 90mm.

FIGHTING COMPARTMENT REAR WALL

Armoured firing port plug and viewing device.

The engine deck cover and mounting bolts.

The loader's hatch and distinctive twin ventilator fan "bell housings".

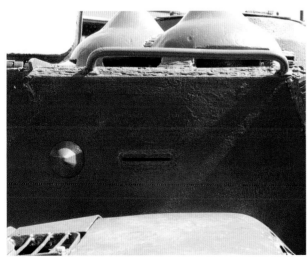

Fighting compartment rear wall with vision device and firing port plug.

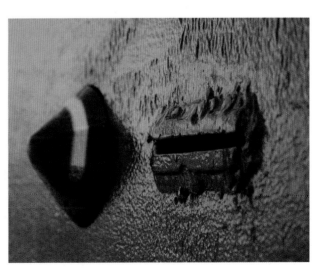

Vision device and firing port plug in close-up.

FIGHTING COMPARTMENT ROOF

The new 670x650mm "panorama" (gunner's) hatch type as installed from May 1945.

"Panorama hatch" torsion bar.

The "panorama" hatch and viewing device.

The Mk. 4 viewing device.

The "panorama" gunner's hatch in open position.

The hatch had a raised hatch coaming for weather protection.

Panorama hatch, left side, in open position.

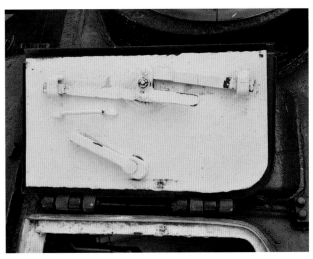

Panorama hatch, right side, in open position.

The armoured "bell" ventilator fan covers.

The ventilator fan covers and desant handrail.

The circular ventilator fan covers were foreshortened and welded together.

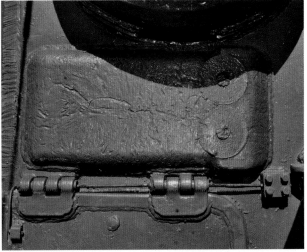

The armoured cap over the internally mounted detent (gun clamp) latched in transit.

FIGHTING COMPARTMENT ROOF

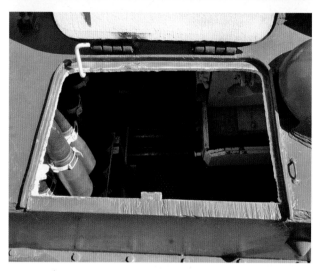

The 760x570mm loader's hatch as used from May 1945.

Loader's hatch with torsion bar.

The later loaders and panorama hatches featured unified four section hinges (previously six).

Note the hatch stop and lock mountings which differ from earlier wartime production SU-100s.

FIGHTING COMPARTMENT SIDE WALLS

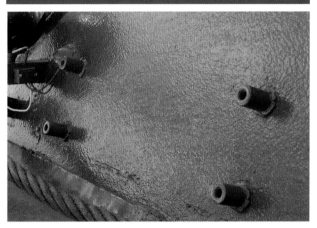

Personal weapons firing port armoured plug, right side of vehicle.

MZA-3 fuel transfer pump storage box mountings from the 1960s.

The mounting points for the MZA-3 fuel pump stowage box are a standard post-war feature. The welded canvas cover tie-points are non-standard.

The scars where the secondary desant handrail was mounted and later removed are evident in this view.

DRIVER'S HATCH

The driver-mechanic's hatch is similar to the hatch of the T-34 tank, but the internal mounting is slightly different.

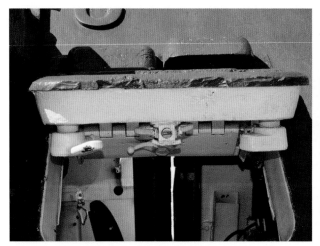

Driver-mechanic's hatch cover with locking bolts.

Driver-mechanic's hatch, showing the lock bolts and handle.

Armoured vision device covers, side view.

Overhead view, five section hatch hinge and armoured vision device covers.

Engine radiator exhaust grille with twin internal louvres.

The lightly armoured grille hinged upwards for inspection.

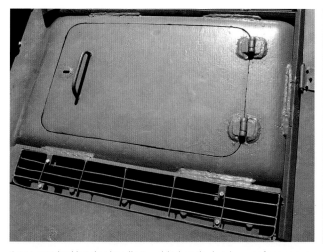

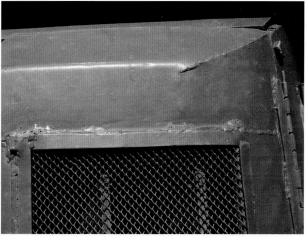

A non-standard bracket-handle is welded on the hatch cover for access to the engine.

Note welding seams on the lightly armoured grille cover assembly.

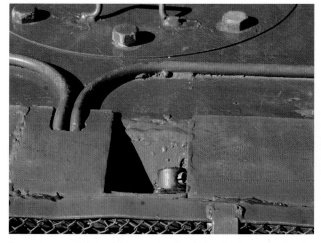

Rear red convoy light and the post-war electrical socket for connecting the MZA-3 fuel pump are placed in this cutout.

Oil filler armoured cover. Note the non-standard offset desant handrail welding.

EXTERNAL FUEL TANKS

Post-war fuel tanks and the engine tools and spares ZIP container.

Wartime mounting brackets, but late post-war 90 litre fuel containers.

Late post-war type "universal" 90 litre fuel containers.

External fuel tank brackets as used from January 1945.

These late post-war "universal" fuel tanks were also used on the IS-3M and ISU-152K/M. The relocated filler cap aided fuel drainage when required.

Tow cable strap tie point.

GLACIS PLATE
& FRONT LOWER PLATE

A firing port embrasure with gutter. The original armoured plug has been lost and the embrasure welded over, common on museum exhibits.

Frontal fuel tanks - fuel filler armoured cap.

UZTM Plant production №711977.

This welded plate denotes planned post-war repairs.

Cover for the right track tensioner mechanism. This protrudes further than normal on this example.

The later butt-welded glacis joint without a beam section.

REAR PLATE & DRIVE HOUSING

Traces of 1960s rebuild. These mounting brackets are for the 200 litre fuel barrels.

Red rear convoy light, and post-war electrical socket for MZA-3 fuel transfer pump.

Single section rear armoured plate hinge bracket.

Six section transmission inspection plate hinge.

Exhaust and armoured exhaust cover.

Exhaust cover and post-war 200 litre barrel mounting bracket.

This SU-100 was at one time fitted with two 200 litre "long-range" fuel tanks.

Side view of the mountings for the 200 litre "long-range" fuel tanks.

The substantial cast final drive housing (right side)

Post-war 200 litre barrel mounting bracket.

There are two types of final drive oil level check and refill plugs as described in the text, protruding and countersunk.

GUN & MANTLET

The cast fixed and moving parts of the gun mantlet.

Overhead view of the gun mantlet. The rain guard is stamped sheet steel.

The mantlet embrasure for the gun sight.

The eyelet was for installing and for removing the armament including the gun mantlet.

The cast gun mantlet had a distinctive brow on the left side.

Gun mantlet with the distinctive cast grooves allowing access to the mounting bolts with power tools. The groove castings varied as described in the main text.

The moving part of the gun mantlet has a distinctive mounting bolt pattern.

The sheet steel gun mantlet rain guard.

The barrel rifling on the 100mm D-10S gun.

The gun barrel has an unobtrusive strengthening collar.

The Padikovo museum's SU-100 on display during an open day. The substantial length of the gun barrel is evident.

WHEELS & SUSPENSION

Typical solid disc road wheels with late type hub bearing caps.

Typical wheel damage.

Wheel tyre / rim moulding, 830x150 (mm).

Post-war hub bearing cap after post-war rebuild.

Wartime SU-100s were fitted with solid disc wheels as they left the manu-facturing plant.

Drive sprocket with later type "assymetrical bonok" roller bearing covers.

Drive sprocket wheel.

Inner side of drive sprocket showing inner end of roller bearing pin (bonok).

The bearing caps were castellated nuts on early production SU-100s.

Idler wheel.

UZTM wheel balance limiters were welded at an angle rather than being vertical.

TRACKS

The SU-100 used standard T-34 "waffle" tracks. Note the grouser attachment holes.

Track shoe with guide horn, as fitted on every alternate shoe.

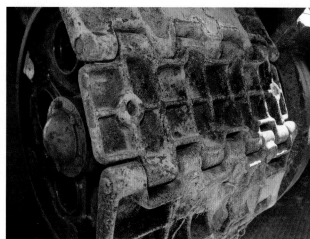

Track link with retainer pin.

Cast "waffle" track with grouser attachment holes.

Glacis with direct butt-welded armour sections and five spare links. Ex-works, seven links were fitted as standard.

TOWING HOOKS & WIRE

Glacis towing hook and tow cable latch.

The spring loaded tow hook latch.

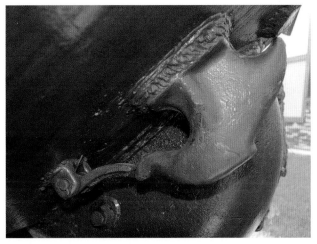

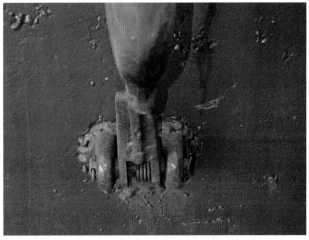

Rear tow hook and spring loaded latch mechanism.

Close-up view of spring loaded latch mechanism.

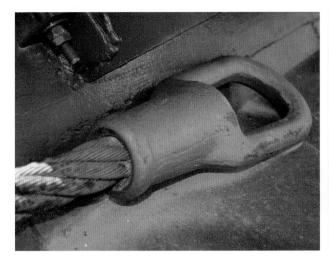

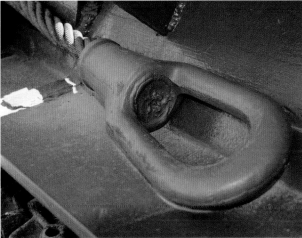

The tow cable thimbles are post-war and not original to the SU-100.

Most SU-100s in museums have non-original tow cables fitted.

MUDGUARDS

UZTM never fitted these angular track guards, which were a 1950s modernisation.

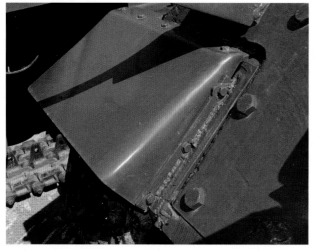

Rear track guards.

Post-war box for spare parts for engine and tools. Longitudinal strengtheners recognise it.

Track grousers, three stacks of six per the plant drawings.

The grousers were held in place by canvas straps and buckles.

HEADLIGHT, HORN & ANTENNA FOOT

FG-105 post-war headlight.

The signal horn is not original to the SU-100, dating from the 1980s.

The headlight and signal horn mountings.

Post-war ASh-4 antenna pot for post-war R-120 or R-123 radio set.

The armoured ASh-4 antenna pot.

Overhead view of the ASh-4 antennna pot mounting.

DRIVER MECHANIC'S POSITION

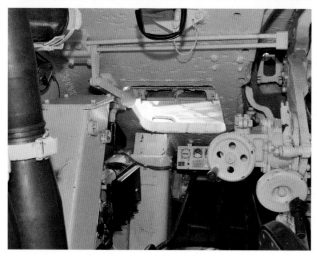

Driver-mechanic's position with open hatch.

Due to the size of the 100mm D-10S gun, the driver-mechanic's position was particularly tight on the SU-100.

Driver-mechanic's instrument panel (post-war modification).

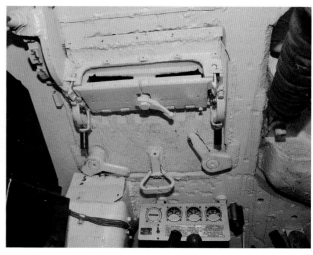

Driver-mechanic's position with hatch closed.

Hatch release handle and modernised post-war TPU communications system switch.

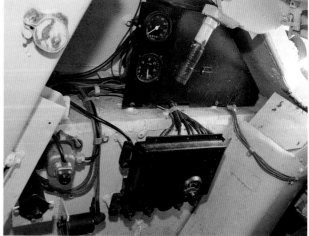

Post-war electric panel.

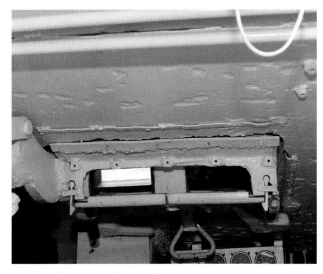

Driver-mechanic's vision devices, left device open.

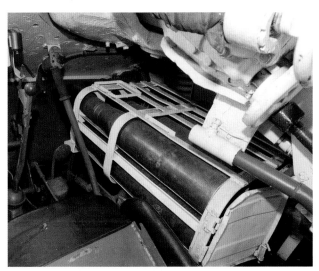

Rack for 8 rounds in the forward fighting compartment.

Left side track tensioning device.

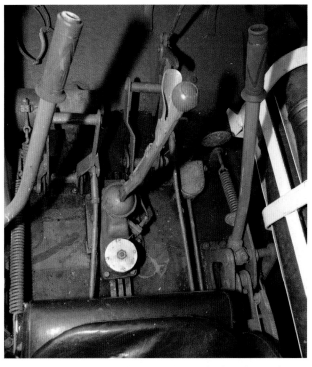

Driver-mechanic's position with steering levers, clutch, brake, accelerator and gear linkage.

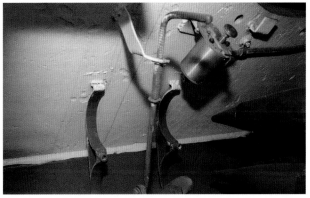

Clamps for two compressed air cylinders (engine start).

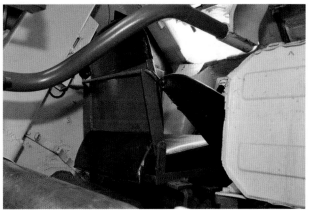

Driver-mechanic's position.

COMMANDER'S POSITION

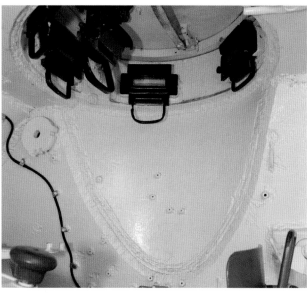

R-123 "Magnolia" or R-123M post-war power supply (left) R-124 TPU commander's panel for R-124 radio set (right)

Commander's sponson and cupola.

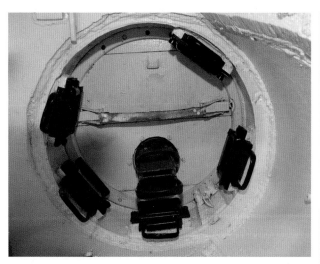

Commander's vision device.

Early commander's cupola with split leaf hatch.

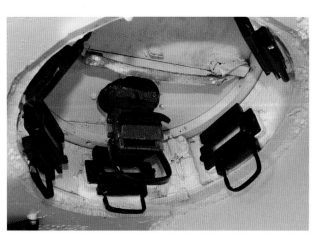

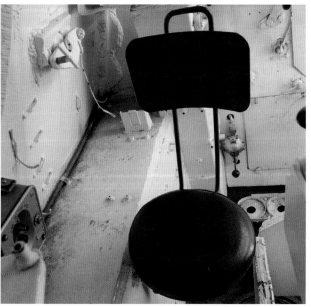

Commander's cupola with Mk.4 periscope and vision devices.

Commander's seat.

AMMUNITION

Six rounds were stowed on the sloping left fighting compartment wall.

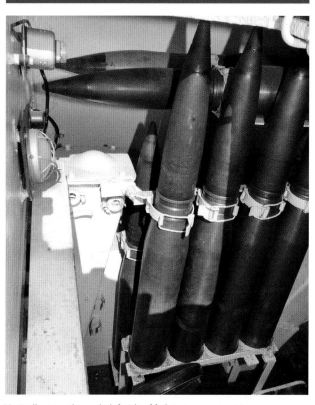

Vertically stowed rounds, left side of fighting compartment.

Rack for eight rounds - forward fighting compartment.

Rounds were secured by metal latches.

Two rounds clamped to the hull floor under the gun.

Container for eight rounds, forward fighting compartment.

FIGHTING COMPARTMENT

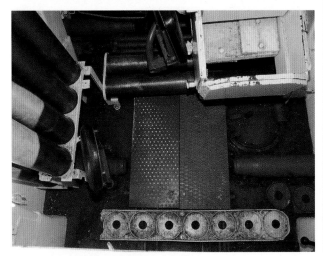

Empty vertical stowage rack for seven rounds.

Escape hatch under the commander's seat.

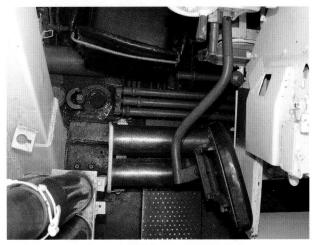

Rounds were stowed where space allowed, not always ideal for the loader.

Rounds latched to their floor mounted rack.

The SU-100 had two forward fuel tanks (painted orange), one mounted above the other.

Upper forward fuel tank and suspension cover.

Radiator air inlet opening lever (left) (located on both sides of the SU-100) and transmission compartment exhaust louvre opening lever (right).

Seven round rack, between fighting compartment and engine compartment wall.

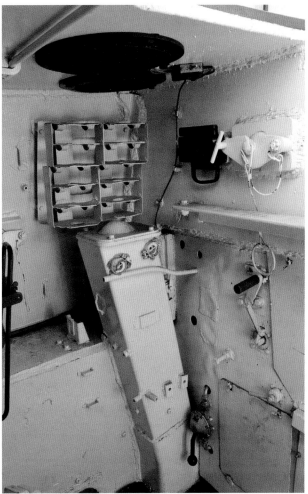

The DT machine-gun disc rack.

Fighting /engine compartment bulkhead.

FIGHTING COMPARTMENT

Exhaust fan grilles. The bell housings accomodated the motors so the fans did not protrude into the fighting compartment.

The gun detent lock in its stowed and locked position.

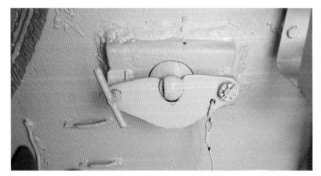

The pistol port armoured plugs were held in place by a metal retainer plate and T-bar lock. When released the plug was retained by a chain (not connected in this photo).

Panorama sight hatch.

Gun detent located in stowed position in the fighting compartment roof.

The driver-mechanic's pistol port, with the chain connected to the armoured plug.

One of the internal lamps with guard.

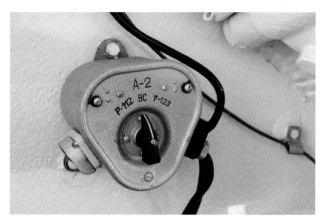

R-112 TPU / R-123 (R-123M) radio switch.

Radio location and radio / TPU switch.

RNM- 1KU-2 manual oil pump.

Suspension spring cover within the fighting compartment.

The SU-100 is painted gloss white internally. Note the hatch torsion spring arm.

ARMAMENT

Ispection stamps on the gun breech showing a manufacture date of 1946.

The welded recoil guard.

Gun mantlet underside view.

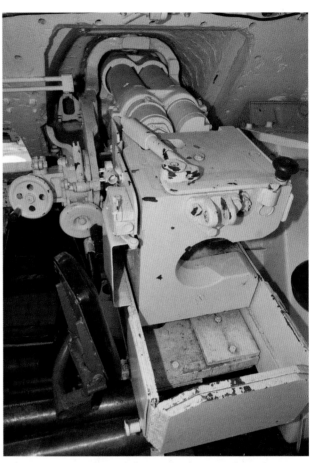

The wedge type gun breech of the 100mm D-10S.

100mm D-10S gun breech with operaing lever.

Gun breech.

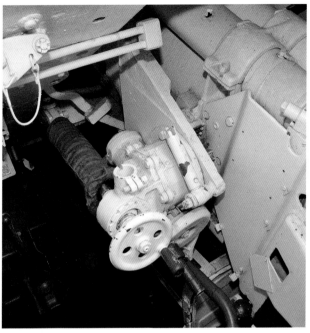

Elevation and travesre controls, overhead view.

View of the armament installation from the driver-mechanic's position.

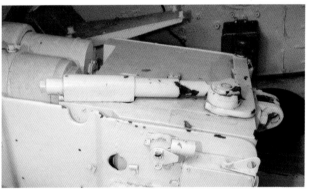

Gun breech, overhead view.

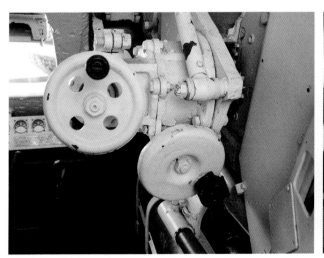

Elevation and traverse wheels.

Canvas shroud covering the cantilevered mechanism.

Chapter 10

Preserved SU-100 & SD-100 vehicles

The SU-100 entered service with the Red Army only six months before the end of the war, but was engaged in the final push into Axis territory and towards Berlin in the early spring of 1945. The SU-100 suffered some significant losses during its short service, but by the time of its service introduction the Red Army had long-since been on the offensive, and this combined with the "over watch" role of the SU-100 resulted in SU-100 attrition rates being relatively low overall.

The SU-100 continued in production at UZTM (Sverdlovsk) in the immediate post-war era, with small-scale production undertaken post-war at Plant №174 (Omsk), The SU-100 was also manufactured post-war in Czechoslovakia as the SD-100, and widely exported by both the Soviet Union and Czechoslovakia. Domestically, the SU-100 was standardised as a close-support vehicle in the immediate post-war Soviet

Army and was upgraded several times, remaining in Soviet service into the early 1970s. There are as a result many surviving SU-100s to be found in museums worldwide, though many are Czechoslovakian export SD-100 vehicles. The "default" museums of Aberdeen, Bovington and Saumur located in the United States, Great Britain and France respectively have had SU-100s (actually SD-100s) in their collections for decades. In Israel, there are examples located in Tel Aviv and Latrun, while there are SU-100s to be found in museums in most former Soviet Bloc and Warsaw Pact countries, in China, South Korea and many other countries around the world. There are also surviving examples to be found mounted on plinths as war memorials in the Belarus, the Russian Federation and Ukraine.

The SU-100 also continues to be used at major anniversary parades on Moscow's Red Square, with seven restored vehicles,

This SU-100 with the early wartime commander's cupola was one of seven restored SU-100s paraded through Red Square during the 75th anniversary Victory Parade on Red Square on 24th June 2020. The vehicle has the post-war angular track guards, fuel transfer pump stowage container and later driving and running lights, but has otherwise been restored back to wartime configuration. (Russian Ministry of Defence)

including wartime built examples, being paraded in the Russian Federation in 2020, more than 75 years after they were originally built.

In recent years, there has been an increase in the number of SU-100s being added to museum collections in the Russian Federation, with these sometimes being modified back to wartime configuration with reference to the original manufacturer's production drawings. The example located at the Museum of Russian Military History located at Padikovo near Moscow is one such vehicle in the process of "retro-restoration" to original configuration; with the internal restoration giving an enti-

rely fresh perspective on how these vehicles looked in original combat order.

In 2020, the SU-100 is a relatively common exhibit in military museums around the world. Most examples located outside the former Soviet Bloc are however post-war or Czechoslovakian manufacture, and nearly all museum exhibits have been modified and reconfigured from their original build specification. The following examples are however indicative of the number of preserved SU-100s to be found in museums around the world, , and also in "active service" during Russian commemorative parades.

An SU-100 at the 2nd Guards Tamanskaya Motorised Rifle Division base at Alabino during Victory Day parade rehearsals in 2010. The vehicle has typical 1950s and 1960s upgrades, including the fuel transfer pump container behind the commander's cupola and the "starfish" roadwheels. (Aleksandr Koshavtsev)

A column of SU-100s at the 2nd Guards Tamanskaya Division base at Alabino rehearsing for the 2010 Victory Parade on Moscow's Red Square. (Aleksandr Koshavtsev)

This SU-100 belonging to the Kubinka Tank Museum has a mix of post-war upgrades including the late hand tool stowage arrangement and a non-standard driving light configuration. Note also the later road wheels on the first and last wheel stations. Kubinka 70th anniversary show 14th July 2001.

This image of an UZTM built SU-100 being unloaded from a KamAZ-65225 tank transporter during an evening parade rehearsal in 2010 provides a good view of the rarely observed upper surface details of the vehicle.

SU-100s parked near the Central Telegraph building in central Moscow await an evening rehearsal for the 9th May 2010 Victory Parade.

A column of wartime era production SU-100s move on to Red Square for the 75th anniversary Victory Parade held on 24th June 2020.
(Vera Chervonyaschaya)

PRESERVED SU-100 & SD-100 VEHICLES

Country	City or Town	Location	Description
Australia	Cairns, Queensland	Australian Armour and Artillery Museum	SU-100 restored in Bulgaria
Austria	Vienna	Museum of Military History (Arsenal Museum)	Wartime specification SU-100 without posr-war upgrades
Belarus	Baran (Vitebsk Oblast)		SU-100 plinth mounted as a war memorial
	Beshankovichy (Vitebsk Oblast)	Military Technical Museum	SU-100
	Brest	Brest Fortress Museum	SU-100
	Gomel	Museum of Military Glory	SU-100
	Maryina Horka (Minsk Oblast)		SU-100 plinth mounted as a war memorial
	Minsk	Great Patriotic War Museum	SU-100, now located within the newly reconstructed museum buildings
		Military Academy	SU-100
	Prudok (Gomel Oblast)		SU-100 plinth mounted as a war memorial
	Vitebsk	Memorial Park	SU-100
	Zaslavl, near Minsk	Stalin Line Museum	2 restored SU-100a, one running, and a wreck
		Stalin Line Museum	Mounted as a memorial on the main road Minsk-Warsaw
Bulgaria	Sofia	National Museum of Military History	SD-100 (2 examples)
China	Dan Dong	Korean War Museum	
	Nanhai Foshan (Guandong Province)		
	Yangfang	Chinese Tank Museum	Three SU-100s ex PLA service
Czech Republic	Lesany	Army Technical Museum	SD-100 (2 examples)
	Rokycany	Demarcation Line Museum	SD-100
	Zdice	Army Museum	SD-100
	Zovo	Zovo Air Park	SD-100 (2 examples)
Cuba	Havana	Museum of the Revolution	Plinth mounted monument
	Playa Guron (Bay of Pigs)	Museo de la Intervencion	SU-100s plinth mounted as memorials
Egypt	Cairo	October War Panorama Museum	SD 100
France	La Wantzenau	Military Museum	SD-100 in running condition. Ex Ardennes Military Museum, Belgium
	Saumur	Musee des Blindés (Saumur Tank Museum)	SD-100 captured at Port Said, Egypt, 1956. White camouflage paint in diorama setting
Georgia	Adjura		SU-100 plinth mounted as a war memorial
Germany	Berlin	Karlshorst	
	Dresden	Military Museumof the Bundeswehr	SU-100
	Munster	Munster Panzer Museum	SD-100
	Ravensbrück	Former Concentration Camp	SU-100 mounted on a brick plinth commemorating liberation by the Red Army
Great Britain	Duxford	Imperial War Museum	Czech built SD-100 captured by 3rd Battalion, Parachute Regiment, Suez, 1956
	Wareham, Dorset	Tank Museum, Bovington	Czech built SD-100 captured by 3rd Battalion, Parachute Regiment, Suez, 1956
	Coventry	Private collection, former Alvis facility	Ex Budge collection
Holland	Heidenau	Private collection (Jorn Bindig)	SD-100
	Nijverdal	Staman Industrial Trading premises	Private collection. Ex Ukraine
Hungary			
Israel	Kiryat Shimona	Memorial Complex	SD-100 (display of 3 SD-100s)
	Latrun	Yad La-Shiryon Museum	SD-100
	Tel Aviv	Israeli Defence Forces Tank Museum	SD-100
Jordan	Amman	Royal Jordanian Tank Museum	SU-100 in Russian markings
Latvia	Svente	Auto-Retro Museum	SU-100
Mongolia	Ulan Bator	Military Museum	SU-100
	Saynshand		SU-100 mounted on a concrete plinth as a memorial
	Ondorhaan		SU-100 mounted on a plinth together with a BT-5 fast tank
Poland	Poznan	Military History Museum	SU-100 in running order
Romania	Bucharest	Museum of Military History	SD-100, ex Romanian Army
	Orastie	Arsenal Park Transylvania	Two SD-100s

For regularly updated information on preseved SU-100 and other Soviet AFVs the authors recommend the websites: www.preservedtanks.com and www. the.shadock.free.fr

Russian Federation	Alushta (Crimea)		SU-100 plinth mounted as a war memorial
	Belgorod	Kursk Battle Museum	SU-100
	Chelyabinsk	Memorial park	SU-100
	Chita	Siberian Military District Headquarters Building	SU-100
		Victory Park	SU-100
	Ekaterinburg	Gate Guardian in front of Uralmash (UZTM) plant	SU-100 mounted on a granite plinth infront of the manufacturing plant as a war memorial
	Kubinka	Kubinka Tank Museum	1 SU-100 in running order currently at Patriot Park 1 Gate Guardian together with a T-34-85
	Moscow	Central Armed Forces Museum	SU-100
		Memorial Complex, Paklonnaya Gora (Victory Park)	2 SU-100s in scenic settings
		Mosfilm Studios	SU-100 in running order
		Strogino Region	SU-100 installed as a war memorial
	Arkhangelskoe (Moscow Oblast)	Muzei Tekhniki (Vadim Zadorozhny Museum)	SU-100 in running order
	Chornogolovka	Muzei Tekhniki Chernogolovka	SU-100 built on an SU-85 chassis, formerly a war memorial within the territory of a military institute
	Lenino-Snegiri (Moscow Oblast)	Memorial Museum Complex	SU-100 Plant No174 (Omsk) production
	Padikovo	Museum of Russian Military History	SU-100 in running order
	Sholokovo (Moscow Oblast)	T-34 Museum	SU-100
	Krasnodar	Great Patriotic War Memorial Park	SU-100
	Murmansk	Museum of the Air Forces of the Northern Fleet	SU-100
	Mylino (Nizhny Novgorod Oblast)		SU-100
	Omsk	Omsk Battle Glory Museum	SU-100
	Padikovo (Moscow region)	Museum of Russian Military History	Fully restored and equipped SU-100 in running order
	Penza	Memorial park	SU-100
	Pinozero (Murmansk Oblast)		SU-100
	Prokharovka (Belgorod Oblast)	Battle of Kursk memorial Museum	Several SU-100s in an open setting
	Safonovo (Murmansk Oblast)		SU-100 plinth mounted as a war memorial
	Sapun Gora (Crimea)	Sapun Gora Memorial Museum	Restored to running condition. Local victory parade participant
	St. Petersburg	Artillery, Engineering and Engineer Forces Museum	SU-100
	Ulyanovsk	Memorial park	SU-100
	Ussuriysk	Military Academy	SU-100 on a brick plinth. Mix of wheel types
	Verkhnyaya Pyshma	Battle Glory of the Urals Military Museum	SU-100 with post-war upgrades
	Voronezh	Defence of Voronezh Panorama Memorial Park	SU-100 (2)
Slovakia	Dargov		SD-100 mounted on a plinth
	Pivka	Park of Military History	SD-100
	Svidnik	Military Museum	SD-100
South Korea	Seoul	Seoul War Museum	
Ukraine	Alchevsk (Lugansk Oblast)		SU-100
	Bilozerka (Kherson Oblast)		SU-100 plinth mounted as a war memorial
	Izium (Kharkiv Oblast)		SU-100
	Kiev	Great Patriotic War Memorial Museum	SU-100 (3 examples)
	Makeeva (Donetsk Oblast)		SU-100 plinth mounted as a war memorial
	Novyy Buh (Mykolaiv Oblast)		SU-100 plinth mounted as a war memorial
	Odessa	411 Battery Museum Park	
	Rivne		SU-100 plinth mounted as a war memorial (30th anniversary of liberation 1944-1974)
	Saurov (Donetsk Oblast)		SU-100 plinth mounted as a war memorial
	Shatsk (Volyn Oblast)		SU-100 plinth mounted as a war memorial
	Sofia Borschchakovka (Kiev Oblast)		SU-100
	Storozhynets (Chernivtsi Oblast)		SU-100 plinth mounted as a war memorial
	Vapniarka (Vynnitsia Oblast)		SU-100 plinth mounted as a war memorial
	Vishnjaki (Poltava Oblast)		SU-100 plinth mounted as a war memorial commemorating liberation 19th September 1943
United States	Aberdeen	Aberdeen Proving Grounds	SD-100, recently removed
	Anniston, Alabama	US Army Military history Storage Centre	SD-100, ex Aberdeen Proving Ground
	Hudson, Maine	American Heritage Museum	SU-100, ex Jacques Littlefield collection
	Fort Benning, Georgia	US Armour and Cavalry Collage, Fort Benning	SD-100
Vietnam	Hanoi	Museum of Armoured Forces	
	Ho Chi Minh	War Remnants Museum	

ABERDEEN PROVING GROUND

The SD-100 pictured was captured during the (British - French) Suez crisis in 1956 and exported to the United States where it was on display at the famous Aberdeen Proving Ground collection for many years. (Steven J. Zaloga)

BERLIN KARLSHORST

The former Red Army headquarters building in Berlin Karlshorst, where the German surrender was delivered and accepted in 1945 has a small collection of wartime armoured vehicles including this SU-100.

BOVINGTON

The ex Egyptian SD-100 located at the Bovington Tank Museum in England was captured by the 3rd Battalion, Parachute Regiment - "3 Para" - in Port Said, Egypt during the Suez crisis of 1956. The SD-100s located in the Imperial War Museum, Duxford, England, Saumur in France and formerly at Aberdeen Proving Ground in the United States were all captured during the same engagement.

BUCHAREST (ROMANIA)

This SD-100 is located at the Military History Museum in Bucharest, Romania.

CAIRO
This SU-100 is located at the October War Panorama Museum in Cairo, Egypt. (Aleksandr Morzhitsky)

CHITA (RUSSIA)
This SU-100 is located in the eastern Siberian city of Chita.

CHELYABINSK (RUSSIA)

This SU-100, located at Victory Park in Chelyabinsk is in almost wartime configuration, albeit with minor post-war changes such as removed grab handles and non-original track guards. (Andrey Malyshev)

KIRYAT SHIMONA (ISRAEL)

This war memorial, consisting of three brightly painted SD-100s, is located at Kiryat Shimona in Israel

CHERNOGOLOVKA (MOSCOW OBLAST)

This "SU-100" at the Muzei Tekhniki in Chernogolovka is an example of how vehicles can radically change appearance in their post-service life. Formerly plinth mounted on the territory of a military academy, this is actually an original SU-85 chassis mounting a post-war D-10SK gun and mantlet.

KIEV

The Great Patriotic War Memorial Museum in Kiev has three SU-100s on display though not all are correctly described.

KRASNODAR (RUSSIA)

This SU-100, with original roadwheels and post-war crew personal effects and fuel transfer pump containers is located at the 30ᵗʰ Anniversary of Victory in memorial park in Krasnodar in southern Russia.

KRASNOGORSK (MOSCOW OBLAST)

The SU-100 at the Muzei Tekhniki in Arkhangelskoe, near Krasnogorsk in the western suburbs of Moscow is in the process of being back-dated to wartime specification. The vehicle is in running condition.

VORONEZH (RUSSIA)

The Russian industrial city of Voronezh has a permanent memorial park garden remembering its World War Two history. The vehicle has been fitted with non-original T-54 type mudguards for display purposes but is otherwise original.

MINSK

This SU-100, shown at the old city cente site of the Great Patriotic War Museum in Minsk has now been relocated inside a new and purpose built exhibition building.

ZASLAVL (BELARUS)

This "abandoned" SU-100 is positioned on the "Stalin Line" fortification complex at Zaslavl in modern Belarus. In the summer of 1941, invading Axis forces advanced on the line across the fields in the background.

ZASLAVL (BELARUS)

The Stalin Line Museum at Zaslavl near Minsk has two restored SU-100s within its collection. As with many museum exhibits the gun mantlet rain guard is missing.

MOSCOW

There are two SU-100s located at the Paklonnaya Gora war memorial complex west of Moscow city centre, both located in scenic display settings. The late production widened and single hatch commander's cupola is evident in this view.

MOSCOW

This SU-100 installed as a memorial is located at Strogino, a residential suburb in the west of Moscow.

ODESSA (UKRAINE)

This SU-100 is located at the 411th Battery Museum in Odessa, Ukraine. (Aleksandr Morzhitsky)

OMSK (RUSSIA)

A typical SU-100 with post-war upgrades including a mix of early T-34 "spiderweb" wheels and post-war "starfish" wheels on display at the Battle Glory Museum in Omsk.

KUBINKA (PATRIOT PARK)

Tanks and other armoured vehicles from Kubinka are now regularly rotated through the nearby Patriot Park exhibition complex.

ROVNO (UKRAINE)

There are a not insignificant number of plinth mounted SU-100s preserved as war memorials in the Russian Federation, Belarus and Ukraine. This example is in the Ukrainian city of Rovno.

SAPUN GORA (CRIMEA)

This SU-100 located at Sapun Gora in Crimea was as with several of the exhibits recently restored to running condition. On 24th June 2020 the vehicle was paraded through the city centre of nearby Sevastopol for the 75th anniversary Victory Parade commemorations, as held throughout the Russian Federation.

SHOLOKOVO (MOSCOW OBLAST)

This SU-100 at the T-34 museum at Sholokovo near Moscow has typical post-war upgrades including a mix of roadwheel types.

SNEGRI (MOSCOW OBLAST)

This Plant №174 (Omsk) production SU-100 is located at the Lenino-Snegiro memorial complex near Dedovsk in the western suburbs of Moscow.

ST. PETERSBURG (RUSSIA)

The SU-100 at the Artillery, Engineer and Communications Forces Museum in St. Petersburg does not have most of the typical post-war modernisations common to the majority of museum examples.

EKATERINBURG

This SU-100, was an early exhibit at the now greatly expanded Urals Military Glory Museum complex at Verkhnyaya Pyshma near Ekaterinburg. The site of the museum is within sight of where the majority of SU-100s, and all wartime production examples, were built. This example is without the post-war personal effects container but has the mountings for the fuel transfer pump box behind the cupola and "starfish" pattern roadwheels added during capital rebuilds.

VIENNA

This ex Red Army SU-100 located at the Museum of Military History (the Arsenal Museum) in Vienna is in original wartime service specification without the upgrades seen on most museum examples. (Margarita Platonova)

YANGFANG (CHINA)

The Chinese Tank Museum located in Yangfang near Beijing has a number of SU-100s on display. (Yuri Pasholok)

TEL AVIV (ISRAEL)

The Israeli Defence Forces History Museum in Tel Aviv has a Czechoslovakian production SD-100 together with many other Soviet Bloc origin vehicles, primarily captured during the Arab-Israeli wars of 1967 and 1973. (Yuri Pasholok)

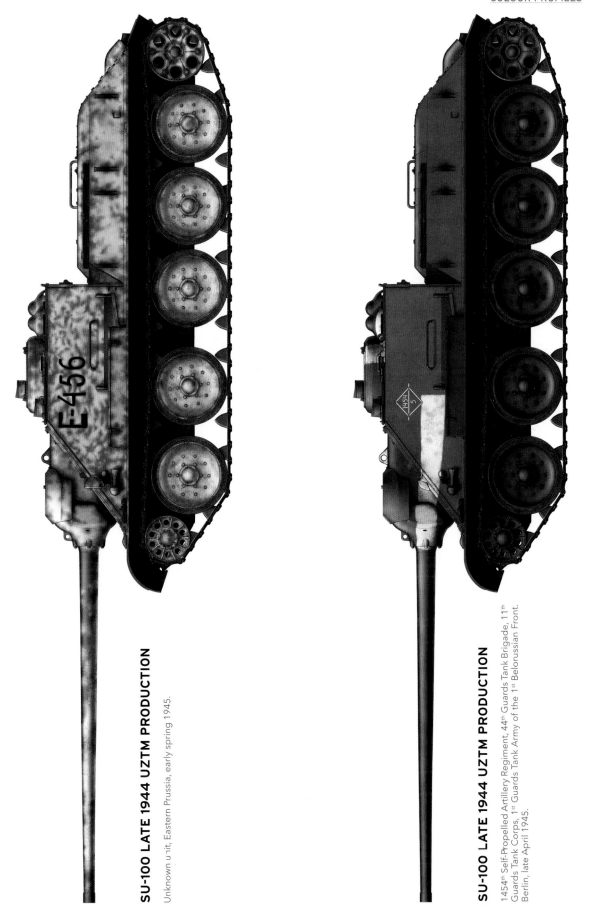

SU-100 LATE 1944 UZTM PRODUCTION

Unknown unit, Eastern Prussia, early spring 1945.

SU-100 LATE 1944 UZTM PRODUCTION

1454th Self-Propelled Artillery Regiment, 44th Guards Tank Brigade, 11th Guards Tank Corps, 1st Guards Tank Army of the 1st Belorussian Front. Berlin, late April 1945.

SU-100 LATE 1944 UZTM PRODUCTION

Probably 1893rd Self-Propelled Artillery Regiment, 6th Guards Tank Corps 3rd Guards Tank Army of 1st Ukrainian Front, Prague, May 1945.

SU-100 LATE 1944 UZTM PRODUCTION

Modernised in the 1960s, of an unknown unit during the "Danube" operation in Czechoslovakia, probably the last action of the SU-100 in Soviet Army service. The white cross as applied over the fighting compartment is for identification of Warsaw Pact forces.

SU-100 POST-WAR OMSK PLANT PRODUCTION

45th Anti-Tank Brigade, 11th Corps of the Army of the Serbian Republic, Eastern Slavonia, 1992. The Serbian tricolor is repeated on both sides, the right side of glacis plate and the loader's hatch.

SU-100 OF JANUARY-FEBRUARY 1945 UZTM PRODUCTION

Modernised in the late 1960s, captured by Houthi rebels from governmental forces during the civil war in Yemen, 2017.

Appendix and Glossary

Glossary

ABTU (АБТУ)	*Avtobronetankovoe Upravlenie (Auto-Tank Command)*
ANIOP	*Artilleriskiy Nauchno-Issledovatelskiy Polygon - Artillery Scientific Experimental Test Range*
ArtKom GAU KA (АртКом ГАУ КА)	*Artillery Committee Main Artillery Command of the Red Army*
BTU (БТУ)	*Bronetankovoe Upravlenie - Tank Command*
DOT (ДОТ)	*Dolgovremennaya Ognevaya Tochka (hardened fire-point)(bunker)*
GABTU KA (ГАБТУ КА)	*Glavnoye AvtoBronetankovoyea Upravlenye KA - Main Auto-Tank Command of the Red Army*
GAU	*Glavnoye Artilleriiskoye Upravleniye - State Artillery Directorate*
GAZ	*Gorky Avtomobilny Zavod - GAZ plant (named after Molotov)*
GKO	*Gosudarstnenny Komitet Oboroni - State Defence Committee of the USSR*
KA (КА)	*Krasnaya Armiya - Red Army (also known as RKKA)*
KB (КБ)	*Konstruktorskoye Bureau - Design Bureau*
KhEMZ	*Kharkov Electromekhanicheskiy Zavod - Kharkov Electromechanical plant*
NATI	*Nationalniy Avtomobilniy Traktorniy Institut (National Auto-Tractor Institute)*
NKAP	*Narkomat Aviatsionnoi Promishlennosti.*
NKO	*Narodny Kommisariat Oboroni - State Defence Committee*
NKV	*People's Commissariat of Armaments*
NKSM	*Ministry of Medium Machine Building (Narkomsredmash) - responsible for tank production*
NKTM	*People's Commissariat of Heavy Engineering*
NKTP	*People's Commissariat of Tank Production*
OF	*Oskolochno-Fugasny - High-Explosive Fragmentation*
RGAEh (РГАЭ)	*Rossiskiy Gosudarstvenniyi Arkhiv Ekonomiki - Российский Государственной Архив - Russian State Economic Archives*
RGASPI (РГАСПИ)	*Rossiskiy Gosudarstvenniy Arkhiv Sotsialno-Politichesko Istorii - Russian State Archive of Social-Political History*
SAU (САУ)	*Samokhodnaya Art. Ustanovka - Self-Propelled Artillery Piece (SAU or SU)*
SNK (СНК СССР)	*Sovet Narodnikh Kommissarov - Council of People's Commissars*
TsaMO RF (ЦАМО РФ)	*Tsentralniy Arkhiv Ministerstva Oboroni Rossiskoi Federatsii - Central Archives of the Ministry of Defence of the Russian Federation*
TsVKP(b) (ЦК ВКП(6)	*Central Committee of the CPSU(b) - Communist Party (Bolshevik) of the USSR*
TTT	*Taktiko-Tekhnicheskiye Trebovaniya - Tactical Technical Tasks*
USA (УСА)	*Upravlenie Samohodnoy Artillerii - Self-Propelled Artillery Department*
Voenizdat	*State Military Publisher NKO SSSR*
VVS KA	*Voenno-Vozdushniye Sili Krasnoi Armii - Red Army Air Force*
ZSU (3СУ)	*Zenitnaya Samokhodnaya Ustanovka - Self Propelled Anti-Aircraft Gun*

Notes

Desant - Literally "landing" troops, a description applied to tank borne infantry and to airborne forces.

Acknowledgements

As with any book, the end result is the input of many people other than the named authors. The authors would like to thank Andrey Aksenov for photographing the Padikovo SU-100 in detail. The specialists that contributed relevant information that helped to build the SU-100 story are mentioned in the text. Thanks also to Peter Plume for his technical input on aspects of T-34 and SU-100 restorations. And as with other books in this series, many thanks to Elizabeth Kinnear for her diligent proof-reading. She particularly enjoyed proofing the technical description chapter…

Soviet Era Place Names

After the break up of the Soviet Union, several cities in Ukraine reverted to use of local Ukrainian language and spelling. The spellings used in this book are consistent with the period in Soviet history being described.

Soviet Ministries

Soviet ministries were abbreviated to NK (Narodny Kommissariat - People's Commissariat) followed by the responsibility, e.g. NKV (Vooruzhenie - armaments), NKSM (Srednie Mashinostroeniye - medium machine building (actually tank production)) etc. The minister was known as the Narkom (Kommissar). Commissariat can be interpreted as Ministry, and Commissar as Minister.

NKAP	*People's Commissariat of Aviation Production*
NKGK	*People's Commissariat of State Control*
NKO	*People's Commissariat of Defence*
NKS	*People's Commissariat of Machine Tool Building*
NKSM	*People's Commissariat of Medium (i.e. Tank) Machine Building*
NKSP	*People's Commissariat of Steel Production*
NKTM	*People's Commissariat of Heavy Engineering*
NKTP	*People's Commissariat of Heavy (i.e. Tank) Production in wartime*
NKTP	*People's Commissariat of Tank Production*
NKV	*People's Commissariat of Armaments*

Soviet Ministries - As written in the original Russian:

НКАП	Наркомат Авиационной промышленности - People's Commissariat of Aviation Industry - NKAP
НКГК	Народный Комиссариат Государственного Контроля - People's Commissariat of State Control - NKGK
НКС	Народный Комиссариат Станкостроению - People's Commissariat of Machine Tool Building - NKS
НКСМ	Наркомат Среднего Машиностроения - People's Commissariat of Medium Machine Building - NKSM
НКТП	Народный Комиссариат Танковой Промышленности - People's Commissariat of Tank Industry - NKTP
НКВ	Народный Комиссариат Вооружения - People's Commissariat of Armaments - NKV
НКТМ	Наркомат Тяжелого Машиностроения - People's Commissariat of Heavy Machine Building - NKTM

Наркомат (Ministry) Народный (People's) are from the same word root, so are effectively interchangeable.

Photographic archives

Andrey Aksenov, Vyacheslav Belogrud, Vera Chervonyaschaya, James Kinnear, RGAKF - Russian State Archive of Cinematic and Photographic Documentation, Mikhail Svirin, Russian Ministry of Defence, TsGAKFF - Central State Archive of Cinematic and Photographic Documentation, Yuri Pasholok, Steven J. Zaloga, Igor Zheltov, Museum of Russian Military History, Padikovo, Moscow.

The authors would like to thank Dmitry Viktorovich Persheev and the staff at the Museum of Russian Military History at Padikovo for their assistance in allowing unrestricted access to their restored SU-100 for the internal photographs used in this book. The museum takes tremendous pride in restoring wartime era Red Army combat vehicles and other equipment to original specification and often to operational condition. This includes outfitting the vehicles where possible with all the peripheral equipment used in service and usually long lost on museum exhibits. Such museum restoration is work is not simply world class but world leading.

Bibliography

The bibliography for this book is relatively short due to the limited level of pre-existing research on the subject. The material used for this book comes almost exclusively from the archives of the Russian State organizations as noted at the beginning of the book , together with contemporary operational and service documentation, manuals, etc.

Books

Baryatinsky, Mikhail, *Sovietskie Tanki v Boyu ot T-26 do IS-2. Eksmo, Moscow, 2007*
Baryatinsky, Mikhail, *Tanki Vtoroi Mirovoi, Eksmo, Moscow, 2009*
Drig, Evgenniy, *Mekhanizirovannie Korpus RKKA v Boyu, Transkniga, Moscow, 2005*
Kosirev,E.A, Orekhov, E.M, Fomin, N.N, *Tanki, Izdaletstvo DOSAAF, Moscow, 1973*
Solyankin, A.G, Pavlov, M.V, Pavlov, I.V, Zheltov, I.G, *Otechestvennie Bronirovannie Mashini XX vek Tom 2 1941-45. Eksprint, Moscow. 2005*
Svirin, Mikhail, *Tanki Stalinsky Epokhi, Yauza, Eksmo, Moscow, 2001*

Journals & Magazines

MHobby, Tekhnika i Vooruzhenie, Tekhnika Molodezhi

Author Biographies

James Kinnear was born in Great Britain and has researched the topic of Soviet and Russian military hardware since his first visit to the enigmatic and mysterious Soviet Union as a young teenager. Having first visited the country when it was considered a threat, and all who travelled there as tourists were scrutinised as suspect communists back home in Blighty (rather than perhaps just having an appreciation for beautiful women), James subsequently lived and worked in the post-Soviet Russian Federation throughout the entire period of post-Soviet "stability" - the two decades between the Soviet Union being considered a military threat and the Russian Federation finding itself again categorized as such again in recent history.

James has written hundreds of articles on Soviet and Russian military technology. A Russian speaker, he has studied the subject from within the military intelligence community and as a civilian author. He is a formal contributor to IHS Jane's defence yearbooks and has published books on Soviet military technology with Barbarossa, Darlington, Osprey Vanguard and Tankograd. This is his fifth book for Canfora Publishing.

Nikolai Polikarpov is the chief editor of "M-Hobby", the first and only Russian monthly magazine for military modellers, which has been in publication since 1993. The founding of the magazine was a natural extension of his hobby of building scale models. The desire to build models which were an exact replica of the original full scale prototypes naturally led to the study of the development and operational history of military vehicles during World War Two, including archive research and the measurement of preserved museums examples. This led to the publication of numerous reference articles in "M-Hobby", and also a series of Russian books and monographs regarding the history of Soviet combat and transport vehicles. The publishing of books and articles led to membership of the Union of Journalists of Russia and ongoing work in popularizing military history in various publications.

The SU-100 was last displayed in Moscow as late as the year this book was published, with seven SU-100s paraded across Red Square commemorating the 75th anniversary of the end of World War Two in Europe and the Soviet Victory Parade held on 24th June 1945. (Vera Chervonyaschaya)